Year-Round

A Comprehensive Guide to Growing Fresh, Organic Produce in Your Garden Throughout the Year for a Healthier Lifestyle and Self-Sufficiency

By Sandra Soleil

Table of Contents

Chapter 1: Introduction to Year-Round Vegetable Gardening 5

   Benefits of year-round gardening 10

   Overcoming seasonal limitations 14

   The joy and satisfaction of growing your food 18

Chapter 2: Planning Your Year-Round Garden ... 24

   Assessing your climate and growing conditions 28

   Selecting the right vegetables for each season 32

   Creating a planting schedule and rotation plan 37

Chapter 3: Soil Preparation and Organic Fertilization 43

   Understanding soil composition and pH 47

   Building healthy soil through composting and organic amendments 52

   Using natural fertilizers and soil conditioners 55

Chapter 4: Starting Seeds and Transplants 60

   Choosing the right seeds and varieties 64

   Starting seeds indoors and outdoors 69

   Transplanting seedlings for optimal growth .. 73

Chapter 5: Cultivation Techniques for Each Season 79

Spring gardening: preparing for the growing season 85

Summer gardening: managing heat and water requirements 90

Winter gardening: strategies for cold-weather gardening 100

Chapter 6: Pest and Disease Management 105

Identifying common garden pests and diseases 109

Natural and organic pest control methods 114

Companion planting and beneficial insects .. 118

Chapter 7: Innovative Gardening Methods 124

Container gardening: maximizing space and portability 128

Raised beds and vertical gardening: optimizing growing areas 133

Hydroponics and aquaponics: soilless gardening techniques 138

Chapter 8: Extending the Growing Season 143

Using season extenders like cold frames, row covers, and hoop houses 147

Protecting plants from frost and extreme temperatures 151

Harvesting techniques for mature and immature crops 156

Chapter 9: Harvesting and Storing Your Produce 161

  Harvesting vegetables at their peak flavour and maturity 166

  Proper washing, drying, and storage methods 169

  Canning, freezing, and drying techniques for preserving your harvest 175

Chapter 10: Enjoying Your Year-Round Harvest 181

Chapter 1: Introduction to Year-Round Vegetable Gardening

Year-round vegetable gardening refers to growing vegetables throughout the year, regardless of the season. Traditionally, vegetable gardening has been associated with the spring and summer seasons when temperatures are warmer and more conducive to plant growth. However, with advancements in gardening techniques and the availability of various tools and technologies, it is now possible to grow vegetables all year, even in colder climates.

The concept of year-round vegetable gardening is based on the understanding that different vegetables have different temperature and light requirements for optimal growth. By carefully selecting the right varieties of vegetables and providing them with the ideal conditions, gardeners can extend their harvest season and enjoy a continuous supply of fresh, homegrown produce.

To achieve year-round vegetable gardening, several techniques and strategies can be employed:

1. Season Extension: One of the primary methods used in year-round vegetable gardening is season extension. This involves using techniques such as cold frames, greenhouses, row covers, and cloches to

protect plants from frost and cold temperatures. These structures trap heat and create a microclimate that mimics a warmer season, allowing plants to thrive even in colder months.

2. Succession Planting: Succession planting involves sowing or planting crops at regular intervals to ensure a continuous harvest. By staggering plantings, gardeners can avoid a large harvest all at once and instead have a steady supply of vegetables throughout the year. As one crop is harvested, another is planted in its place, maximizing available space and resources.

3. Indoor Gardening: Indoor gardening, also known as container gardening or hydroponics, allows for vegetable cultivation in controlled environments, such as a sunny windowsill, a spare room, or a dedicated indoor garden setup. With proper lighting, temperature control, and nutrient supplementation, a wide range of vegetables can be grown indoors regardless of the outdoor weather conditions.

4. Crop Selection: Choosing the right crops is crucial for year-round vegetable gardening. Some vegetables are more cold-tolerant and can be grown during colder months, while others thrive in warmer weather. Gardeners can ensure a continuous harvest by selecting

a diverse range of crops and varieties suitable for each season.
5. Organic Soil Management: Maintaining healthy soil is essential for the success of any gardening endeavour, including year-round vegetable gardening. Using organic fertilizers, compost, and practising crop rotation helps replenish nutrients in the soil and prevents the buildup of pests and diseases, leading to healthier plants and higher yields.

Year-round vegetable gardening offers numerous benefits. It provides a sustainable source of fresh produce, reduces food miles and carbon footprint, and allows gardeners to connect with nature throughout the year. Moreover, it offers the satisfaction of self-sufficiency and the opportunity to experiment with a wider variety of vegetables.

It's important to note that the specific techniques and strategies for year-round vegetable gardening may vary depending on your climate, available resources, and gardening preferences. It's always recommended to consult local gardening experts, extension offices, or experienced gardeners in your area for personalized advice and guidance.

Some additional points to consider when it comes to year-round vegetable gardening:
1. Climate Considerations: Understanding your local climate is crucial for successful year-round vegetable gardening. Different

regions have varying temperature ranges, frost dates, and daylight hours. Research the specific climate conditions in your area and select vegetables well-suited to your climate zone. You may also need to adjust or modify your gardening techniques based on your local conditions.

2. Temperature Management: Maintaining the right temperature is essential for year-round vegetable gardening. In colder months, using insulation materials such as straw or blankets around plants can provide additional protection. Employing heating systems, such as radiant heaters or heating cables, can also help maintain optimal temperatures in greenhouses or indoor setups during winter.

3. Light Management: Adequate light is crucial for plant growth. During the darker months of the year, supplementing natural light with artificial lighting, such as grow lights, can ensure that plants receive the necessary amount of light for photosynthesis. Understanding the light requirements of different vegetables will help you provide the appropriate lighting conditions.

4. Watering and Irrigation: Consistent and appropriate watering is vital for the health of your plants. Be mindful of the watering needs of different vegetables and adjust your watering schedule accordingly. Consider

using efficient irrigation systems, such as drip irrigation or soaker hoses, to minimize water wastage and deliver water directly to the plant roots.

5. Pest and Disease Management: Just like in traditional gardening, pests and diseases can affect year-round vegetable gardens. Regular monitoring, early detection, and implementation of preventive measures, such as proper sanitation, crop rotation, and organic pest control methods, will help minimize the risk of infestations and diseases.

6. Crop Protection: In addition to pests and diseases, other elements like extreme weather, strong winds, and heavy rain can damage crops. Using structures like windbreaks, shade cloth, or netting can protect against these elements, ensuring the safety and well-being of your plants.

7. Continuous Learning: Year-round vegetable gardening is a dynamic process that requires continuous learning and experimentation. Keep records of your gardening activities, note successes and failures, and learn from your experiences. Stay updated with gardening resources, attend workshops, and connect with fellow gardeners to expand your knowledge and improve your skills.

Remember, year-round vegetable gardening may have challenges, but it also offers great rewards.

With proper planning, suitable techniques, and dedication, you can enjoy a bountiful harvest of fresh, homegrown vegetables throughout the year. Happy gardening!

Benefits of year-round gardening

Year-round gardening refers to cultivating plants and crops throughout the year, regardless of seasonal limitations. This approach offers several benefits, both practical and environmental. Here are some advantages of year-round gardening:

1. Continuous food production: One of the primary benefits of year-round gardening is the consistent supply of fresh produce. By growing crops throughout the year, you can enjoy a diverse range of fruits, vegetables, and herbs regardless of the season. This can lead to better nutrition, reduced reliance on grocery stores, and increased self-sufficiency.
2. Extended growing seasons: Traditional gardening methods often rely on specific growing seasons, limiting the time available to cultivate plants. Year-round gardening, on the other hand, enables you to extend the growing season by creating controlled environments. This can be achieved through techniques such as indoor gardening, greenhouses, and cold frames or season-

extending techniques like row covers and mulching.
3. Improved plant health: Consistent care and attention to plants throughout the year can improve plant health. With year-round gardening, you can closely monitor and manage factors such as water, light, temperature, and nutrient levels. By providing optimal conditions, you can minimize the risk of pests, diseases, and other environmental stressors, leading to healthier and more robust plants.
4. Higher crop yields: With year-round gardening, you can maximize your garden's productivity. By staggering plantings and utilizing space efficiently, you can increase the overall yield of your crops. Additionally, you can experiment with different varieties and growing techniques to find what works best for your specific environment, resulting in higher crop yields over time.
5. Environmental sustainability: Year-round gardening promotes environmental sustainability in multiple ways. Firstly, by reducing reliance on long-distance transportation and commercial agriculture, you contribute to lower carbon emissions associated with food production and transportation. Secondly, growing your food allows you to avoid pesticides and chemical fertilizers, promoting organic and

sustainable practices. Lastly, year-round gardening encourages biodiversity, as you can create habitats for beneficial insects and pollinators, contributing to the ecosystem's overall health.

6. Therapeutic and recreational benefits: Gardening has been shown to have therapeutic effects, reducing stress, promoting relaxation, and improving mental well-being. Year-round gardening provides a continuous outlet for these benefits, allowing you to engage in a fulfilling and enjoyable hobby throughout the year. It can also be a great way to stay physically active and spend time outdoors, connecting with nature and enjoying the rewards of your efforts.

7. Cost savings: Growing your food year-round can lead to significant cost savings over time. By producing your fruits, vegetables, and herbs, you can reduce your grocery bills and avoid the price fluctuations associated with seasonal produce. Additionally, the initial investment in gardening equipment and infrastructure, such as greenhouses or raised beds, can be offset by long-term savings on store-bought produce.

8. Educational opportunities: Year-round gardening provides a rich learning experience, particularly for children. It offers an opportunity to teach them about

plant life cycles, sustainable practices, nutrition, and the importance of environmental stewardship. They can actively participate in planting, nurturing, and harvesting crops, fostering a sense of responsibility and connection to the natural world.

9. Flexibility and variety: With year-round gardening, you have the flexibility to grow a wide variety of crops. You can experiment with different types of fruits, vegetables, and herbs, including heirlooms or exotic varieties that may not be readily available in stores. This allows you to diversify your diet, try new flavours, and explore culinary possibilities.

10. Local and seasonal eating: Year-round gardening supports the principles of eating locally and seasonally. By growing your food, you can align your diet with what is naturally available and thrive in your region at any given time. This can lead to a greater appreciation for local flavours, reduced carbon footprint, and support for local biodiversity.

11. Community engagement: Year-round gardening can foster community engagement and collaboration. By sharing your gardening knowledge and excess produce with neighbours, friends, or local community organizations, you can

strengthen social connections and contribute to food security initiatives. Community gardens and shared gardening spaces can become hubs for education, social interaction, and collective problem-solving.

12. Personal fulfilment and satisfaction: Engaging in year-round gardening can bring a sense of personal fulfilment and satisfaction. Witnessing the growth and progress of your plants, enjoying the flavours of your harvest, and knowing that you have contributed to your food production can be immensely gratifying. Gardening also provides an opportunity to connect with nature, reduce stress, and find a sense of peace and purpose.

These additional benefits further highlight the advantages of year-round gardening, offering an array of reasons to embrace this practice and enjoy its rewards.

Overcoming seasonal limitations

"Overcoming seasonal limitations" refers to finding ways to mitigate or minimize the challenges and restrictions posed by changing seasons. Various activities, industries, and aspects of life can be affected by seasonal variations, and overcoming these limitations involves implementing strategies or solutions to ensure continuity, efficiency, and productivity regardless of the season.

Here are a few examples of how different areas may address seasonal limitations:

1. Agriculture: Agriculture heavily relies on seasons for crop growth, and farmers face challenges when seasons change. To overcome these limitations, farmers can adopt techniques such as greenhouse cultivation, hydroponics, or vertical farming, which provide controlled environments and allow year-round cultivation. They can also use techniques like crop rotation and choose specific crop varieties suited for different seasons.
2. Tourism: Some tourist destinations may experience low visitor numbers during specific seasons. To overcome this, they may develop alternative attractions or events that are appealing during off-peak periods. For instance, ski resorts may offer activities like hiking or mountain biking in the summer to attract visitors during the warmer months.
3. Retail: Retail businesses often experience fluctuations in demand based on seasons. To overcome this, they can diversify their product offerings to cater to different seasonal needs. For example, clothing stores may stock winter wear during colder months and swimwear during summer,

ensuring they have products suitable for each season.
4. Energy: Seasonal limitations can impact energy production, particularly in regions with extreme climate variations. To overcome this, renewable energy sources like solar and wind can be used alongside conventional sources to maintain a stable energy supply throughout the year. Energy storage technologies, such as batteries, can also help store excess energy during high production seasons for use during low production seasons.
5. Construction: Seasonal variations, especially in areas with harsh winters, can limit construction activities. To overcome this, construction companies may plan projects to utilize favourable seasons and techniques that enable construction in colder climates. These techniques include using heated enclosures, insulating materials, and employing specialized equipment suited for cold weather conditions.
6. Food Preservation: Certain fruits and vegetables are only available during specific seasons. To overcome the limitations of seasonal availability, preservation techniques like canning, freezing, and drying can be employed. This allows the consumption of seasonal produce

throughout the year and reduces reliance on imported or out-of-season items.

7. Seasonal Employment: Some industries, such as agriculture and tourism, experience fluctuations in labour demand based on seasons. To address this, businesses can offer training programs or skill development initiatives to attract workers during off-peak seasons. Additionally, they may diversify their operations or collaborate with other industries to create year-round employment opportunities.

8. Seasonal Allergies: Many individuals suffer from allergies during specific seasons, such as spring or fall. To overcome the limitations of seasonal allergies, people can take preventive measures like regularly cleaning their living spaces, using air purifiers, wearing protective masks when necessary, and taking medication or seeking medical treatment to manage symptoms.

9. Seasonal Dependent Sports: Sports and recreational activities dependent on specific seasons, such as skiing or snowboarding, face limitations during other times of the year. To overcome this, indoor alternatives or variations of these activities can be developed. For instance, indoor ski slopes or synthetic ice rinks allow enthusiasts to participate in these activities regardless of the season or climate.

10. Seasonal Marketing Campaigns: Businesses often create marketing campaigns tailored to specific seasons or holidays. To overcome limitations, companies can design flexible marketing strategies that incorporate elements from different seasons or focus on evergreen themes that resonate with consumers year-round. This allows for consistent brand messaging and engagement, irrespective of the season.

These examples demonstrate how individuals, industries, and businesses can find creative solutions to overcome seasonal limitations. By adapting practices, implementing new technologies, and utilizing alternative approaches, we can minimize the constraints imposed by changing seasons and ensure continuous progress and efficiency throughout the year.

The joy and satisfaction of growing your food

1. Connection with nature: Growing your food allows you to engage directly with the natural world. You become intimately connected with the seasons, weather patterns, and the life cycles of plants. This connection can foster a sense of appreciation for the Earth's resources and a

greater understanding of the delicate balance required for plants to thrive.
2. Fresh and flavorful produce: Nothing quite like the taste of freshly picked fruits, vegetables, and herbs from your garden. Homegrown produce often has superior flavour, as it is allowed to ripen fully on the vine or tree rather than being harvested prematurely for transport. The vibrant flavours and aromas can elevate your culinary experiences and make meals more enjoyable.
3. Nutritional benefits: Growing your food gives you control over the cultivation process, allowing you to choose which seeds to plant and which farming practices to follow. You can prioritize organic and sustainable methods, avoiding harmful pesticides and synthetic fertilizers. This can result in more nutritious and healthier food options for you and your family.
4. Physical and mental well-being: Gardening is a physically active hobby that can provide exercise and fresh air. It offers an opportunity to get outside, soak up some sunlight, and engage in gentle movements like planting, weeding, and harvesting. These activities can be therapeutic and help reduce stress, anxiety, and depression. Gardening also encourages mindfulness and

a sense of accomplishment, boosting overall mental well-being.

5. Self-sufficiency and sustainability: Growing your food promotes self-sufficiency by reducing reliance on external sources. It empowers you to take charge of your food supply and reduces the need for extensive transportation, packaging, and processing that often come with store-bought produce. By cultivating your food, you contribute to a more sustainable lifestyle and minimize your carbon footprint.

6. Educational opportunities: Gardening offers a wealth of learning experiences. Whether you're a beginner or an experienced gardener, there is always something new to discover. You can learn about plant biology, soil health, pest control, and various gardening techniques. Sharing this knowledge with others, particularly younger generations, can instil a deeper appreciation for food, nature, and the importance of sustainable practices.

7. Community building: Gardening can bring people together, fostering a sense of community. Community gardens, for instance, provide shared spaces where individuals can cultivate their plots and interact with fellow gardeners. It's an opportunity to exchange knowledge, tips, and surplus produce. Participating in or

supporting local farmers' markets and seed swaps can also strengthen community ties and promote a sense of collective well-being.
8. Cost savings: Growing your food can be a cost-effective alternative to buying produce from the store. While there are initial investments in gardening supplies and seeds, long-term savings can be significant, especially if you have a productive garden. This is particularly true for expensive or speciality items you can grow at home, such as herbs, gourmet vegetables, or exotic fruits.
9. Environmental impact: When you grow your food, you can implement environmentally friendly practices that reduce your impact on the planet. By avoiding chemical pesticides and fertilizers, you contribute to the health of local ecosystems and protect beneficial insects and pollinators. Additionally, you can compost kitchen scraps and yard waste, reducing waste sent to landfills and creating nutrient-rich soil amendments.
10. Food security: In a world where food availability and prices can be unpredictable, growing your food can provide a sense of security. Whether it's a small backyard garden or a larger plot, having access to homegrown produce gives you control over your food supply. It can also be empowering

to know that you have the skills and resources to nourish yourself and your loved ones.

11. Sense of accomplishment and empowerment: Seeing the fruits of your labour grow and thrive can be incredibly satisfying. The process of nurturing a tiny seed into a flourishing plant and harvesting the resulting product provides a sense of accomplishment and pride. Gardening can also boost self-confidence and empower individuals to take charge of their well-being and sustainability.

12. Creativity and experimentation: Growing your food allows for experimentation and creativity in the garden. You can try new plant varieties, explore different growing techniques, and experiment with companion planting or vertical gardening. This freedom to innovate and adapt fosters a sense of curiosity and encourages continuous learning and improvement.

13. Sharing and giving back: When your garden produces an abundance of food, you can share the harvest with others. Sharing homegrown produce with friends, family, neighbours, or local food banks not only promotes community connections but also enables you to contribute to the well-being of others. It's a way to spread the joy and

satisfaction of growing your food and promoting healthy eating habits in your community.

In summary, the joy and satisfaction of growing your food encompass various aspects, including cost savings, environmental impact, food security, accomplishment, empowerment, creativity, sharing, and giving back. Gardening provides:

- A holistic experience beyond cultivating plants.
- Offering numerous benefits for individuals.
- Communities.
- The planet.

Chapter 2: Planning Your Year-Round Garden

Planning your year-round garden involves carefully selecting and organizing your plants and gardening activities throughout the different seasons of the year. It allows you to maximize your garden's productivity and enjoy fresh produce and beautiful blooms all year long. Here are some key steps to help you plan your year-round garden:

1. Determine your gardening goals: Start by clarifying what you want to achieve with your garden. Do you want to focus on growing vegetables, herbs, flowers, or a combination of these? Understanding your goals will help you choose the right plants and plan your garden layout accordingly.

2. Assess your climate and growing conditions: Knowing your local climate and the specific conditions in your garden is crucial for successful gardening. Consider factors such as temperature range, frost dates, sunlight exposure, soil quality, and water availability. This information will guide your plant selection and help you determine which plants thrive in your area during each season.

3. Research suitable plants: Look for plants that are well-suited to your climate and growing conditions. Pay attention to their growth habits, maturity times, and specific care requirements. Consider annuals and perennials to ensure a continuous supply of products or blooms throughout the year.
4. Plan your garden layout: Create a garden layout that optimizes space and maximizes sunlight exposure. Group plants with similar needs together and consider factors like companion planting, succession planting, and crop rotation. Companion planting involves placing plants that benefit each other nearby, while succession planting ensures a continuous harvest by planting new crops as others finish. Crop rotation helps prevent the buildup of pests and diseases by changing the location of crops from one year to the next.
5. Create a planting schedule: Develop a planting schedule that outlines when to sow seeds, transplant seedlings, and harvest crops for each season. Consider the specific growth requirements of your chosen plants and plan accordingly. Take into account the average frost dates in your area and adjust your schedule accordingly to ensure plants are started and harvested at the right times.
6. Provide proper care: Throughout the year, ensure your plants receive adequate water,

nutrients, and protection from pests and diseases. Regularly monitor your garden, make necessary adjustments to watering and fertilizing routines, and promptly address any signs of pests or diseases.
7. Maintain and adapt your garden: As the seasons change, your garden will require ongoing maintenance. Prune, weed, and remove spent plants to keep your garden tidy and healthy. Stay flexible and adapt your plans based on weather conditions, unexpected challenges, or new gardening opportunities.

By following these steps, you can create a year-round garden that provides beauty, fresh produce, and a fulfilling gardening experience throughout every season. Happy gardening!

Here are some additional considerations and tips for planning your year-round garden:
1. Extend the growing season: To maximize your garden's productivity, consider using techniques that extend the growing season. This can include using cold frames, row covers, or even a greenhouse to protect plants from frost and provide them with extra warmth during cooler months. These structures can help you start planting earlier in the spring and continue growing later into the fall or even through the winter, depending on your climate.

2. Choose a variety of plants: Incorporate a mix of plants with different growth patterns and maturity times. Select early, mid-season, and late varieties of vegetables so you have a staggered harvest throughout the year. This ensures a continuous supply of fresh produce. Additionally, include plants with different bloom times to enjoy a variety of colours and fragrances in your garden.
3. Consider vertical gardening: If you have limited space, vertical gardening can be a great solution. Utilize trellises, fences, or stakes to vertically grow climbing plants such as beans, cucumbers, or tomatoes. This maximizes your growing area and allows you to grow more plants in a smaller space.
4. Practice proper soil management: Healthy soil is essential for successful gardening. Before planting, test your soil's pH and nutrient levels to determine if any amendments are needed. Add compost, organic matter, or fertilizers to improve soil fertility. Additionally, consider implementing mulching techniques to conserve moisture, suppress weeds, and regulate soil temperature.
5. Preserve and store your harvest: To enjoy the bounty of your garden year-round, consider preserving your harvest. Canning, freezing, drying, or fermenting fruits, vegetables, and herbs allows you to enjoy

them during the off-season. Research preservation methods and ensure you have the necessary equipment and supplies to store your produce properly.
6. Keep a garden journal: Maintaining a garden journal can be invaluable for tracking your progress, documenting successes and failures, and planning for future seasons. Note important dates, plant varieties, pest and disease occurrences, and any adjustments or improvements you make. This information will help you refine your gardening techniques and make better decisions in the future.

Remember, gardening is an ongoing learning process, and it's essential to stay curious, adapt to challenges, and experiment with new plants and techniques. Enjoy the journey and the rewards of tending to your year-round garden!

Assessing your climate and growing conditions

Assessing your climate and growing conditions refers to evaluating the environmental factors and characteristics of a specific location to determine its suitability for different types of plants, crops, or gardening activities. This assessment is essential for understanding the local climate, soil quality, sunlight exposure, temperature range, precipitation patterns, and other relevant factors that can influence plant growth and development.

Here are some key aspects to consider when assessing climate and growing conditions:

1. Climate: Start by understanding the general climate of your region. This includes the average temperature range throughout the year, seasonal variations, and the length of the growing season. Different plants thrive in different climate types, such as tropical, temperate, arid, or cold climates.
2. Hardiness Zone: Hardiness zones are geographical regions that provide information about the average minimum winter temperature in a specific area. They help determine which plants can survive and thrive in a particular zone. The United States Department of Agriculture (USDA) has developed a hardiness zone map widely used for reference.
3. Sunlight: Assess the amount of sunlight your location receives throughout the day and at different times of the year. Most plants require a certain amount of direct or indirect sunlight to grow properly. Some plants, like vegetables, typically need full sun exposure, while others, such as ferns, can tolerate shade.
4. Soil Quality: Evaluate the composition and quality of your soil. Factors to consider include soil pH, nutrient content, drainage,

and texture (e.g., sandy, loamy, clay). Conducting a soil test can provide valuable information about its fertility and any necessary amendments or adjustments to optimize plant growth.
5. Water Availability and Rainfall Patterns: Consider the availability of water in your area and the regularity of rainfall. Some plants require consistent moisture, while others are drought-tolerant. Understanding the local rainfall patterns and water availability can help you plan irrigation systems and select plants well-suited to your conditions.
6. Microclimates: Investigate if your property has any microclimates, which are localized areas within a larger climate zone with unique environmental conditions. Factors such as topography, proximity to bodies of water, or the presence of buildings or trees can create microclimates with different temperature ranges or wind patterns. These microclimates may enable the cultivation of plants that wouldn't typically thrive in the surrounding area.
7. Frost Dates: Determine the average dates of the last spring frost and the first fall frost in your region. Knowing these dates helps you plan your planting schedule, as certain plants are sensitive to frost and need to be planted after the risk of frost has passed.

8. Wind Patterns: Assess the prevailing wind patterns in your area. Strong winds can impact plant growth, causing damage or drying out the soil. Consider using windbreaks, such as hedges or fences, to protect your plants from excessive wind exposure.
9. Elevation: Take into account the elevation of your location. Higher elevations generally experience cooler temperatures and different weather conditions compared to lower elevations. This can affect the types of plants that can thrive in your area.
10. Pest and Disease Pressure: Research common pests and diseases in your region. Different areas may have specific issues that could affect plant health. Understanding the potential pests and diseases can help you choose plant varieties that are more resistant or take appropriate preventive measures.
11. Pollinator Presence: Assess the presence of pollinators in your area, such as bees, butterflies, or birds. Pollinators play a crucial role in plant reproduction. Providing a habitat and food source for pollinators can enhance the success of your garden or farm.
12. Local Regulations: Familiarize yourself with any local regulations or restrictions related to gardening, farming, or land use. Some areas may have specific

guidelines or permits required for certain activities or practices.

13. Historical Climate Data: Access historical climate data for your region, including temperature and rainfall patterns over several years. This information can give you insights into long-term trends and variations, helping you make more accurate predictions and adapt your gardening strategies accordingly.

Remember, climate and growing conditions can vary even within relatively small geographical areas, so it's important to assess your specific location and its unique characteristics. Consider consulting with local agricultural extension offices, gardening communities, or experienced growers in your area to gather additional insights and advice tailored to your region.

Selecting the right vegetables for each season

Selecting the right vegetables for each season is an important aspect of gardening and cooking. It ensures that you choose vegetables that thrive in the current weather conditions and are more likely to yield a successful harvest. Here's an explanation of how to select the right vegetables for each season:

1. Spring:

- In spring, temperatures start to warm up, and the soil becomes workable. It's a great time to plant cool-season vegetables that can tolerate light frosts, such as lettuce, spinach, kale, radishes, peas, and carrots.
- These vegetables prefer cooler temperatures and can germinate and grow well during this time. They often bolt or turn bitter if exposed to high heat, so it's best to harvest them before the summer heat sets in.

1. Summer:
    - High temperatures and longer days characterize summer. Many vegetables thrive in these conditions, but choosing heat-tolerant varieties is crucial.
    - Tomatoes, peppers, cucumbers, zucchini, beans, eggplant, and corn are popular summer vegetables. They require full sun, warm soil, and consistent watering to grow successfully.
    - Some leafy greens like Swiss chard and certain herbs such as basil can also do well in summer if provided with enough shade and moisture.
1. Fall:
    - Fall is an excellent time for growing cool-season vegetables again. As the

temperatures start to cool down, you can plant crops that prefer milder weather and can tolerate light frosts.
- Vegetables like broccoli, cauliflower, Brussels sprouts, cabbage, beets, turnips, and various salad greens (arugula, kale, mustard greens) are ideal for fall gardening.
- These vegetables mature in cooler fall temperatures, resulting in improved flavour and texture.

1. Winter:
   - Winter gardening varies depending on your climate. In milder regions, you can continue growing many cool-season vegetables from the fall. However, it might be more challenging to grow crops outdoors in colder areas with frost or snow.
   - To extend the growing season, you can use techniques like cold frames, hoop houses, or indoor gardening to grow cold-tolerant vegetables such as winter greens (kale, collards, Swiss chard), carrots, leeks, and radishes.

Here are some additional considerations when selecting vegetables for each season:

1. Soil Preparation:
   - Before planting, it's important to prepare the soil properly. This includes removing weeds, loosening the soil,

and adding compost or organic matter to improve its fertility and drainage.
- Different vegetables have varying soil preferences. For example, root crops like carrots and beets prefer loose, well-drained soil, while leafy greens like lettuce and spinach thrive in fertile soil with good moisture retention.

1. Sunlight Requirements:
   - Most vegetables require a minimum of 6 hours of direct sunlight each day. When selecting vegetables, consider the sunlight availability in your garden or growing area each season.
   - If you have limited sunlight, choose shade-tolerant vegetables like leafy greens, herbs, and certain root crops that can still grow and produce with less sun exposure.
1. Watering Needs:
   - Proper watering is crucial for vegetable growth and productivity. Some vegetables require consistent moisture throughout the season, while others are drought-tolerant.
   - For example, leafy greens and herbs generally need more frequent watering to prevent wilting, while root crops and some fruiting

vegetables can tolerate drier conditions once established.

1. Succession Planting:
   - Succession planting involves planting vegetables in intervals to ensure a continuous harvest. It's particularly useful for crops with a short harvest window or those that may bolt or decline in quality with prolonged heat or cold.
   - By staggering plantings, you can enjoy a steady supply of vegetables throughout the season. For example, you can sow lettuce seeds every few weeks for a continuous harvest rather than a single large harvest.
1. Variety Selection:
   - Within each vegetable type, there are often multiple varieties available. Consider selecting varieties that are known for their performance in specific seasons or have characteristics suited to your local climate.
   - Look for information on seed packets or plant labels that indicate heat tolerance, cold hardiness, days to maturity, and recommended planting times. This can help you choose the best-suited varieties for each season.

Remember that local climate and regional conditions can vary, so it's advisable to consult local gardening resources, extension services, or experienced gardeners in your area for specific recommendations on vegetable selection for each season.

Creating a planting schedule and rotation plan

Creating a planting schedule and rotation plan is a strategic approach to optimize agricultural productivity and minimize the risks associated with monocropping. It involves carefully planning the timing and arrangement of different crops systematically. Here's an explanation of the process:

1. Assessing soil and climate conditions: The first step is to understand the characteristics of your soil, including its fertility, pH level, and nutrient content. Additionally, you need to consider the local climate, including temperature, rainfall patterns, and frost dates. This information will help you determine which crops are suitable for your area and their ideal growing conditions.
2. Determining crop selection: Based on the soil and climate assessment, select a range of crops that thrive in your conditions and align with your goals. Consider factors such as market demand, crop rotation benefits, and personal preferences. Choose a

combination of annuals, perennials, vegetables, fruits, grains, or legumes that complement each other regarding nutrient needs, growth habits, and pest resistance.

3. Planning the planting schedule: Develop a calendar or timeline that outlines when to sow seeds, transplant seedlings, or start harvesting for each crop. Consider the length of growing seasons, germination periods, and maturity times. You might need to stagger planting times to ensure a continuous harvest or align with market demands. Also, account for potential weather events or regional considerations that could affect planting dates.

4. Implementing crop rotation: Crop rotation involves systematically changing the type of crops grown in specific areas from season to season or year to year. The goal is to prevent the buildup of pests, diseases, and nutrient imbalances that can occur with continuous planting of the same crop. Rotate crops based on their families or characteristics, ensuring that plants with similar nutrient requirements are not grown successively in the same plot.

5. Considering companion planting: Companion planting is the practice of strategically planting different crops together to maximize their growth potential and deter pests. Some plants have beneficial

relationships, such as repelling pests or providing shade and support to neighbouring plants. Research companion planting combinations and incorporate them into your planting schedule to create a symbiotic and diverse ecosystem.
6. Documenting and adjusting the plan: Keep detailed records of your planting schedule and rotation plan, including the specific crops, dates, and locations. Regularly assess the success of each planting cycle, noting any challenges or improvements observed. Make adjustments to the plan based on these evaluations, considering crop performance, market demand, and lessons learned from previous seasons.

Here are some additional details regarding creating a planting schedule and rotation plan:
1. Utilizing cover crops: Consider incorporating cover crops into your rotation plan. Cover crops are grown primarily to protect and enrich the soil rather than for harvest. They can help suppress weeds, prevent erosion, improve soil structure, and add organic matter. Select cover crops that address specific soil needs, such as nitrogen fixation, soil compaction reduction, or weed suppression, and incorporate them into the rotation schedule accordingly.
2. Accounting for crop-specific requirements: Different crops have varying nutrient

requirements and growth habits. When creating your planting schedule, consider each crop's specific needs, such as sunlight exposure, spacing requirements, and soil pH preferences. Ensure that the rotation plan allows for appropriate nutrient replenishment and minimizes the risk of nutrient depletion or imbalances in the soil.
3. Considering pest and disease management: Rotate crops strategically to disrupt the life cycles of pests and diseases. Some insects and pathogens have specific host plants, and by altering the crop arrangement, you can reduce their impact. Additionally, select crop combinations that naturally deter pests or attract beneficial insects for biological pest control. Integrate pest and disease management practices into your rotation plan to maintain a healthy and resilient farming system.
4. Long-term planning and crop diversity: When developing your rotation plan, think about the long-term goals for your farm. Consider factors such as market demand, crop profitability, and sustainability. Aim for a diverse crop rotation that balances profitability, soil health, and environmental stewardship. Including a mix of cash crops, cover crops, and green manure crops can help maintain soil fertility, reduce input

costs, and enhance biodiversity on your farm.
5. Consulting local resources: Seek guidance from local agricultural extension services, farmers' cooperatives, or experienced farmers in your region. They can provide valuable insights into crop suitability, local planting schedules, and successful rotation practices specific to your area. Local resources can also offer information on pest and disease management strategies tailored to your region's challenges and help you adapt your plan accordingly.
6. Adapting to changing conditions: Agriculture is influenced by various external factors, such as climate change, market fluctuations, and evolving consumer preferences. Continuously monitor and assess the changing conditions and adapt your planting schedule and rotation plan accordingly. Remain flexible to incorporate new crops, adjust planting dates, or modify crop combinations to optimize productivity and profitability.

Remember, creating a planting schedule and rotation plan is an iterative process that requires observation, experimentation, and adaptation over time. By implementing these strategies, you can enhance your agricultural practices, promote sustainability, and maximize the potential of your farming operation.

Chapter 3: Soil Preparation and Organic Fertilization

Soil preparation and organic fertilization are important practices in agriculture and gardening that aim to create a fertile and nutrient-rich soil environment for optimal plant growth. These practices involve preparing the soil before planting and using organic materials to provide essential nutrients to the plants.

Soil preparation typically involves several steps to ensure the soil is loose, well-aerated, and free from weeds and debris. Some common soil preparation techniques include:

1. Clearing the area: Remove any existing vegetation, rocks, or debris from the planting area to create a clean space for cultivation.
2. Tilling or digging: Loosen the soil by tilling or digging it with a garden fork or tiller. This process helps break up compacted soil, improves drainage, and allows plant roots to penetrate easily.
3. Removing weeds: Eliminate any existing weeds by hand or using a hoe, weed trimmer, or herbicide. Weeds compete with plants for nutrients and can hinder their growth.
4. Adding organic matter: Incorporate organic matter such as compost, well-rotted manure, or leaf mulch into the soil. Organic

matter improves soil structure, enhances water-holding capacity, and provides essential nutrients to plants.
5. Levelling the soil: Smooth out the soil surface with a rake or levelling tool to ensure even planting and watering.

Organic fertilization involves using natural, organic materials to supply nutrients to plants. These fertilizers are derived from plant or animal sources and are rich in essential elements like nitrogen (N), phosphorus (P), and potassium (K), as well as micronutrients. Here are some common types of organic fertilizers:

1. Compost: Compost is a rich, dark, crumbly substance produced by the decomposition of organic waste materials. It improves soil fertility, enhances nutrient availability, and promotes beneficial soil organisms.
2. Manure: Animal manure, such as cow, horse, or chicken manure, is a valuable source of organic matter and nutrients. It is usually aged or composted before application to reduce the risk of pathogens and weed seeds.
3. Bone meal: Bone meal is made from ground animal bones and is a good source of phosphorus and calcium. It is often used to promote root development and flowering in plants.
4. Fish emulsion: Fish emulsion is a liquid fertilizer made from fish byproducts. It contains nitrogen, phosphorus, and trace

elements and is typically applied as a foliar spray or drench.
5. Blood meal: Blood meal is dried and powdered animal blood, high in nitrogen. It releases nitrogen slowly and is commonly used to boost vegetative growth.

Organic fertilizers provide nutrients gradually and improve soil fertility over time. They also support beneficial soil microorganisms and minimize the risk of chemical runoff and environmental pollution.

Overall, soil preparation and organic fertilization practices work together to create a healthy soil ecosystem, ensuring plants have the necessary nutrients and conditions for optimal growth, leading to improved crop yields and healthier gardens.

Soil preparation and organic fertilization:
1. Soil testing: Before starting soil preparation, it is beneficial to conduct a soil test to determine the soil's pH level and nutrient content. This helps in understanding the specific nutrient requirements of the plants and allows for targeted fertilization.
2. Mulching: Mulching is the process of covering the soil surface with a layer of organic material, such as straw, wood chips, or leaves. Mulch helps conserve moisture, suppress weeds, regulate soil temperature, and gradually break down, enriching the soil with organic matter.

3. Cover cropping: Cover crops are grown between planting seasons to protect and improve the soil. They help prevent erosion, suppress weeds, fix nitrogen from the air, and add organic matter when tilled back into the soil.
4. Crop rotation: Practicing crop rotation involves growing different plant species in a particular area each year. This helps prevent the buildup of pests and diseases, balances nutrient uptake, and improves soil health.
5. Vermicomposting: Vermicomposting is the process of using earthworms to decompose organic waste materials. Worm castings, the rich organic matter produced by the worms, are a nutrient-rich fertilizer that can be added to the soil to enhance fertility.
6. Green manure: Green manure involves growing specific plant species, such as legumes, and incorporating them into the soil while they are still green and actively growing. This practice adds organic matter and nitrogen to the soil.
7. Organic liquid fertilizers: In addition to solid organic fertilizers, there are also liquid organic fertilizers available. These are typically made by steeping organic materials, such as seaweed or compost, in water. They can be applied directly to the soil or used as foliar sprays.

8. Nutrient balance: Organic fertilizers provide a balanced range of nutrients, but it's important to understand the specific nutrient requirements of different plants. Balancing the nutrient ratios and avoiding excessive fertilization is crucial to prevent nutrient imbalances or environmental contamination.

Remember that organic fertilization and soil preparation practices should be adapted to the specific needs of the cultivated plants, the soil type, and the local climate conditions. Regular soil and plant health monitoring is essential to make adjustments as needed and achieve the best results.

Understanding soil composition and pH

Soil composition and pH are important factors that influence the fertility and health of the soil. Understanding these aspects is crucial for various agricultural practices, gardening, and environmental management.

Soil composition refers to the combination and proportion of different materials that make up the soil. These materials include minerals, organic matter, water, and air. The mineral portion of soil is derived from the weathering and decomposition of rocks and minerals over long periods. It consists of various-sized particles, such as sand, silt, and clay. The proportions of these particles determine the soil's texture, which affects its water-holding capacity, drainage, and nutrient availability.

Organic matter in the soil includes decaying plant and animal materials, such as leaves, roots, and microorganisms. It plays a vital role in improving soil structure, moisture retention, nutrient cycling, and microbial activity. Organic matter also acts as a reservoir of nutrients, making them available to plants.

Water and air are essential components of soil composition. Pores or spaces between soil particles hold water and air. The size and distribution of these pores influence soil aeration, water movement, and oxygen availability for roots and soil organisms.

Soil pH is a measure of the acidity or alkalinity of the soil. It is determined by the concentration of hydrogen ions (H+) in the soil solution. The pH scale ranges from 0 to 14, where pH seven is considered neutral. Values below 7 indicate acidic conditions, while values above 7 indicate alkaline conditions. pH affects the availability and uptake of nutrients by plants. Different nutrients have varying solubilities and availability at different pH levels. For example, some nutrients like nitrogen, phosphorus, and potassium are more accessible to plants in slightly acidic to neutral pH ranges.

Understanding soil pH is crucial because it helps determine soil suitability for specific crops or plants. Some plants thrive in acidic soils, while others prefer alkaline conditions. Adjusting the pH makes it possible to create more favourable conditions for plant growth and optimize nutrient availability.

Soil composition and pH can be determined through laboratory testing or field-based methods. Soil testing provides valuable information about nutrient levels, pH, and other soil properties, allowing farmers and gardeners to make informed decisions regarding soil management practices. By understanding soil composition and pH, it becomes possible to address nutrient deficiencies and pH imbalances and improve overall soil fertility, leading to healthier plant growth and improved agricultural productivity.

Here are some additional points related to soil composition and pH:

1. Soil Composition and Nutrient Availability: The soil composition greatly influences the availability of nutrients to plants. Clay soils have a higher nutrient-holding capacity but can be poorly drained, while sandy soils have lower nutrient-holding capacity but better drainage. Understanding the composition helps in implementing appropriate fertilization strategies to replenish essential nutrients.

2. Soil Structure and Tilth: Soil composition affects its structure, which refers to how soil particles are arranged and aggregated. Good soil structure allows for better root penetration, water movement, and air circulation. Organic matter plays a crucial role in improving soil structure by binding soil particles together and creating pore spaces.
3. Soil pH and Microbial Activity: Soil pH affects the activity and diversity of soil microorganisms. Different microorganisms have different pH preferences, and their activity influences nutrient cycling, organic matter decomposition, and soil fertility. Maintaining optimal pH conditions can foster a healthy microbial community and enhance soil biological processes.
4. Acidic Soils and Aluminum Toxicity: Acidic soils can lead to the release of aluminium ions, which are toxic to plant roots at high concentrations. Aluminium toxicity affects root development, nutrient uptake, and overall plant health. Proper soil testing and pH adjustment can help mitigate this issue.
5. Soil Amendments: Understanding soil composition and pH guide the use of soil amendments to improve soil fertility. For example, adding lime to acidic soils raises the pH, making them more suitable for certain crops. Similarly, organic

amendments like compost or manure can enhance soil structure, nutrient content, and microbial activity.
6. pH and Nutrient Interactions: Soil pH influences nutrient availability and interactions. For example, at higher pH levels, certain nutrients like iron, manganese, and zinc may become less available to plants. Monitoring pH levels helps identify nutrient deficiencies or imbalances, enabling targeted nutrient management practices.
7. Soil pH Buffering Capacity: The buffering capacity of soil refers to its ability to resist changes in pH. Soils with high buffering capacity require more significant changes in soil amendments or management practices to alter their pH. Understanding soil buffering capacity helps determine the effectiveness and frequency of pH adjustments.

Farmers, gardeners, and environmental managers can make informed decisions regarding soil management practices, nutrient applications, and crop selection by considering soil composition and pH. This knowledge contributes to sustainable agriculture, optimal plant growth, and environmental stewardship.

Building healthy soil through composting and organic amendments

Building healthy soil through composting and organic amendments is an important practice in sustainable agriculture and gardening. It involves the deliberate addition of organic materials to the soil to improve its fertility, structure, and overall health.

Composting is the process of decomposing organic waste materials, such as food scraps, yard waste, and agricultural residues, into a nutrient-rich substance called compost. Compost is a dark, crumbly material that resembles soil and is a valuable source of organic matter. It is rich in essential nutrients like nitrogen, phosphorus, and potassium, as well as micronutrients necessary for plant growth.

When compost is added to the soil, it enhances its structure by improving its ability to hold water and nutrients. Compost acts as a sponge, retaining moisture and reducing the risk of soil erosion. It also promotes the development of a well-aerated soil structure, allowing roots to penetrate easily and facilitating the exchange of gases between the soil and the atmosphere.

Furthermore, composting enhances the biological activity in the soil. It provides a favourable environment for beneficial microorganisms, earthworms, and other soil organisms, contributing to nutrient cycling and decomposition processes. These organisms break down organic matter, releasing nutrients in forms that plants can readily absorb.

Organic amendments, which can include materials like manure, cover crops, and green manures, are also used to improve soil health. These amendments add organic matter and nutrients to the soil, enhancing its fertility and structure. Manure from livestock and poultry contains valuable nutrients and organic matter that can replenish soil nutrients and improve soil structure.

Cover crops are grown specifically to benefit the soil. They are planted between main crops to protect the soil from erosion, increase organic matter content, suppress weeds, and enhance nutrient availability. When cover crops are incorporated into the soil, they add organic matter and help break up compacted soil.

Green manures are cover crops grown and then tilled back into the soil while still green or shortly after flowering. By incorporating green manures, organic matter is added to the soil, providing food for microorganisms and improving soil structure.

Here are some additional points about building healthy soil through composting and organic amendments:

1. Nutrient Recycling: Composting and organic amendments help to recycle nutrients sustainably. Instead of relying solely on synthetic fertilizers, which can have negative environmental impacts, these

practices utilize organic waste materials to naturally replenish and enrich the soil.
2. Soil pH Balance: Compost and certain organic amendments can help to balance soil pH levels. If the soil is too acidic or alkaline, it can hinder nutrient availability to plants. Incorporating compost and appropriate organic amendments can help neutralize the pH and create an optimal environment for plant growth.
3. Carbon Sequestration: Composting and adding organic matter to the soil contribute to carbon sequestration. As organic materials break down, carbon from the atmosphere is captured and stored in the soil, mitigating the effects of climate change by reducing greenhouse gas emissions.
4. Water Retention and Drainage: Healthy soil with ample organic matter has improved water retention capacity. Compost acts like a sponge, absorbing and holding water, which helps to prevent water runoff and erosion. Additionally, organic amendments can enhance soil structure, allowing for better drainage in areas prone to waterlogging.
5. Disease and Pest Suppression: Incorporating compost and organic amendments into the soil promotes a diverse and balanced microbial community. Beneficial microorganisms can help suppress harmful

pathogens and pests, reducing the need for chemical pesticides and fungicides.
6. Reduced Environmental Impact: Composting and organic amendments support sustainable farming practices by reducing reliance on synthetic chemicals. By minimizing the use of synthetic fertilizers, herbicides, and pesticides, the environmental impact of agricultural activities is reduced, including pollution of water bodies and harm to beneficial insects and wildlife.
7. Long-term Soil Health: Building healthy soil through composting and organic amendments is a long-term investment in soil health and fertility. Over time, the continuous addition of organic matter improves soil structure, enhances nutrient availability, and increases the soil's capacity to support healthy plant growth.

It's important to note that the specific methods and materials used for composting and organic amendments may vary depending on factors such as climate, soil type, and the specific needs of the plants being grown. Consulting local agricultural extension services or experienced gardeners can provide region-specific recommendations for successful implementation.

Using natural fertilizers and soil conditioners

Using natural fertilizers and soil conditioners involves the application of organic materials to enhance soil fertility and overall plant growth. These substances are derived from natural sources, such as plant and animal waste, compost, or mineral deposits, and they provide essential nutrients and improve the physical properties of the soil.

Natural fertilizers supply nutrients to the soil in a form that plants can readily absorb. They typically contain a combination of macronutrients (nitrogen, phosphorus, and potassium) and micronutrients (such as calcium, magnesium, and iron) necessary for plant development. Examples of natural fertilizers include compost, manure, bone meal, fish emulsion, and seaweed extracts. These fertilizers release nutrients slowly over time, providing a steady supply of nourishment to plants without the risk of nutrient leaching or burning.

Soil conditioners, on the other hand, focus on improving the structure and texture of the soil. They enhance water retention, aeration, and nutrient-holding capacity, leading to healthier root systems and improved plant growth. Soil conditioners can be organic materials like compost or peat moss, as well as mineral-based substances like vermiculite or perlite. These additives improve soil quality by loosening compacted soils, increasing drainage in heavy clay soils, and promoting moisture retention in sandy soils.

The benefits of using natural fertilizers and soil conditioners are numerous. Firstly, they help build and maintain soil fertility sustainably, reducing reliance on synthetic fertilizers that can have negative environmental impacts. They also enhance soil biodiversity by providing organic matter that supports beneficial microorganisms and earthworms.

Furthermore, natural fertilizers and soil conditioners contribute to the overall health of plants. By providing a balanced range of nutrients, they promote strong root development, vigorous growth, and increased resistance to pests and diseases. They also aid in producing nutrient-rich crops, resulting in improved flavour, nutritional value, and shelf life of harvested produce.

Here are some additional points regarding the use of natural fertilizers and soil conditioners:

1. Environmental sustainability: Natural fertilizers and soil conditioners are derived from renewable resources and promote sustainable agricultural practices. They help reduce chemical runoff and leaching into water bodies, minimizing water pollution. Additionally, they contribute to reducing greenhouse gas emissions compared to synthetic fertilizers, as they require less energy-intensive production processes.

2. Soil structure and water management: Natural fertilizers and soil conditioners improve soil structure by enhancing its ability to retain water, thus reducing water runoff and soil erosion. They also aid in water penetration and drainage, preventing waterlogged conditions in heavy soils and ensuring adequate moisture in sandy soils. Improving soil structure promotes a healthy root environment and allows for efficient nutrient uptake by plants.
3. Long-term soil health: Regular use of natural fertilizers and soil conditioners helps build and maintain long-term soil health. They increase organic matter content in the soil, which enhances nutrient cycling, improves soil structure, and promotes beneficial microbial activity. This, in turn, contributes to the soil's overall fertility, productivity, and resilience.
4. Reduced chemical inputs: By incorporating natural fertilizers and soil conditioners, growers can minimize their reliance on synthetic chemical inputs, such as fertilizers and pesticides. This reduction in chemical usage can positively affect the environment, human health, and biodiversity while still ensuring an adequate nutrient supply for plants.
5. Cost-effective: Natural fertilizers and soil conditioners can be cost-effective

alternatives to synthetic counterparts, especially for small-scale farmers and home gardeners. Many organic materials used as fertilizers and conditioners can be obtained locally or produced on-site through composting, reducing the need for expensive commercial products.

6. Ecosystem benefits: By promoting healthy soil, natural fertilizers and soil conditioners support diverse ecosystems. They provide habitats and food sources for beneficial insects, earthworms, and soil microorganisms, contributing to natural pest control and nutrient cycling processes.
7. Regulation compliance: The use of natural fertilizers and soil conditioners aligns with organic farming standards and regulations. For farmers aiming to achieve organic certification, these practices are essential for maintaining compliance and meeting the requirements of organic farming systems.

Overall, using natural fertilizers and soil conditioners offers numerous advantages, including environmental sustainability, improved soil health, reduced chemical inputs, and cost-effectiveness. By prioritizing organic and sustainable practices, growers can cultivate healthy crops while minimizing the ecological footprint of their agricultural activities.

Chapter 4: Starting Seeds and Transplants

Starting seeds and transplants refers to growing plants from seeds indoors or in controlled environments before transferring them to their final growing location. This method is commonly used to extend the growing season, get a head start on planting, and ensure optimal growing conditions for delicate or slow-growing plants.

The process typically involves the following steps:

1. Seed Selection: Choose high-quality seeds from reputable sources. Consider factors such as plant variety, growth habits, climate suitability, and any specific requirements.
2. Containers and Growing Medium: Select containers suitable for seed starting, such as trays, pots, or seedling cells. Use a sterile growing medium, like a seed-starting mix or a mixture of peat moss, vermiculite, and perlite, which provides good drainage and aeration for the seeds.
3. Sowing Seeds: Follow the instructions on the seed packet for proper sowing depth and spacing. Make small depressions or furrows in the growing medium, place the seeds in them, and cover them lightly with soil. Label the containers to keep track of the plant varieties.

4. Moisture and Temperature: Seeds need consistent moisture to germinate. Water the containers gently or use a spray bottle to avoid displacing the seeds. Maintain the appropriate temperature for germination, which varies depending on the plant species. Many seeds germinate well at room temperature, while others may require bottom heat or a heated propagator.
5. Light: Most seeds require adequate light to grow properly. Place the containers in a well-lit area or provide supplemental lighting using fluorescent lights, LED grow lights, or specialized plant grow lights. Adjust the light source to maintain a distance of a few inches above the seedlings as they grow.
6. Thinning and Transplanting: Once the seedlings have developed their first set of true leaves, thin them out if they are overcrowded. This involves removing weaker or excess seedlings to provide enough space and resources for the remaining ones to grow strong. Transplant the seedlings to larger containers or separate seedling cells if needed, ensuring they have enough space for root development.
7. Harden Off: Before transplanting seedlings outdoors, gradually acclimate them to the outdoor environment. This process, known as hardening off, involves exposing the

seedlings to increasing amounts of sunlight, wind, and outdoor temperatures over 7-10 days. Start with a few hours outside in a sheltered location and gradually increase the time and exposure.

8. Planting Out: Once the seedlings are hardened off and the outdoor conditions are favourable, it's time to plant them in their final growing location. Prepare the soil by removing weeds and incorporating organic matter or fertilizer if necessary. Dig holes or create furrows according to the recommended spacing for the particular plants, gently remove the seedlings from their containers, and plant them at the appropriate depth. Water thoroughly after planting.

9. Watering: It's important to keep the growing medium consistently moist but not waterlogged. Check the moisture level regularly, and water, as needed, using a watering can or spray bottle to avoid disturbing the delicate seedlings. Water from the bottom by placing the containers in a tray filled with water, allowing the soil to absorb moisture through capillary action.

10. Fertilization: As the seedlings grow, they will require nutrients for healthy development. Start fertilizing them with a diluted liquid fertilizer or organic compost tea once they have a few sets of true leaves.

Follow the recommended application rates and frequency specified for the fertilizer you're using.

11. Air Circulation: Good air circulation helps prevent diseases and strengthens the seedlings. Use a small fan set on a low speed to gently move the air around the seedlings. This also helps stimulate stem and root development, making the plants more resilient.

12. Disease and Pest Control: Keep a close eye on the seedlings for any signs of diseases or pests. Maintain cleanliness by regularly removing any fallen leaves or debris. If necessary, treat the seedlings with organic pest control methods or appropriate fungicides as recommended for specific plant diseases.

13. Transplant Timing: Consider the appropriate time to transplant the seedlings outdoors. This depends on factors such as the plant's maturity, the last frost date in your area, and the recommended outdoor planting time. Consult gardening references or local agricultural extension services for specific guidance on when to transplant each plant species.

14. Succession Planting: To ensure a continuous harvest throughout the growing season, practice succession planting. Start new batches of seeds and transplants at

regular intervals so as one crop nears maturity, the next one is ready to take its place in the garden.
15. Record Keeping: Maintain a gardening journal or use a digital tool to record important information about the seeds and transplants you start. Keep track of sowing dates, seed sources, germination rates, growth progress, and any observations or lessons learned. This information will be valuable for future reference and for improving your gardening techniques.

Remember, the specific requirements for starting seeds and growing transplants may vary depending on the plant species. Always refer to the seed packet instructions or reliable gardening resources for plant-specific guidelines. Happy gardening!

Choosing the right seeds and varieties

Choosing the right seeds and varieties is an important aspect of gardening, farming, and plant cultivation. It involves selecting the appropriate types of seeds and plant varieties best suited for your needs, growing conditions, and goals. Here's an explanation of why this process is crucial and how to make informed choices:
1. Adaptation to Growing Conditions: Different plants have specific requirements regarding temperature, sunlight, soil type,

and moisture levels. By choosing seeds and varieties well-adapted to your specific growing conditions, you increase the chances of success and yield. For example, if you live in a region with a short growing season and cool temperatures, selecting cold-tolerant seeds and varieties with shorter maturity periods would be beneficial.

2. Disease and Pest Resistance: Some plant varieties have natural resistance or tolerance to certain diseases, pests, or environmental stresses. By choosing disease-resistant or pest-resistant varieties, you can reduce the risk of crop loss and minimize the need for chemical interventions. This is particularly important for sustainable and organic gardening practices.

3. Yield and Productivity: Different plant varieties have varying levels of yield and productivity. Some varieties may produce higher quantities of fruits, vegetables, or grains, while others may have better quality or taste. Consider your specific goals, such as maximizing crop yield, focusing on high-quality produce, emphasizing taste and flavour, and selecting seeds and varieties accordingly.

4. Plant Characteristics: Plant characteristics such as size, growth habit, and appearance

can also influence your choice of seeds and varieties. For example, if you have limited space, you may prefer compact or dwarf varieties that take up less room. If you are growing for ornamental purposes, you may prioritize plants with vibrant colours or unique foliage patterns.

5. Succession Planting and Crop Rotation: Planning for succession planting and crop rotation is crucial for maintaining soil health and maximizing productivity. By selecting different varieties with varying maturity dates, you can ensure a continuous harvest throughout the growing season. Additionally, rotating crops helps prevent the buildup of pests and diseases in the soil. Consider the time it takes for each variety to mature and plan your planting schedule accordingly.

6. Local Adaptation and Biodiversity: Choosing seeds and varieties that are locally adapted or native to your region can contribute to the preservation of local biodiversity and help maintain resilient plant populations. Local varieties often have unique traits that make them well-suited to the area's specific climate, soil, and pests. Additionally, supporting local seed sources and heirloom varieties helps preserve traditional knowledge and genetic diversity.

To make informed choices when selecting seeds and varieties, consider consulting gardening guides, seed catalogues, or local agricultural extension offices. These sources can provide valuable information about the characteristics, suitability, and performance of different varieties in your area. Additionally, talking to experienced gardeners or farmers in your community can provide insights and recommendations based on their firsthand experience.

1. Taste and Culinary Uses: If you are growing edible plants, taste and culinary uses are important factors to consider. Different varieties of fruits, vegetables, and herbs can have varying flavours, textures, and uses in the kitchen. Some may be better suited for fresh consumption, while others may be ideal for cooking, preserving, or specific culinary preparations. Consider your preferences and intended uses when selecting seeds and varieties.
2. Pollination Requirements: Some plants require cross-pollination, while others are self-pollinating or do not rely on pollinators. Understanding the pollination requirements of the plants you intend to grow is crucial for ensuring proper seed set and fruit production. If you plan to save seeds for future planting, selecting open-pollinated or heirloom varieties is important to maintain genetic diversity.

3. Availability and Accessibility: Seeds and varieties can vary depending on your location and the specific market or supplier. Consider the accessibility of the seeds you need, including the availability of reputable seed companies, local seed exchanges, or community seed banks. If certain varieties are hard to find, you may need to explore alternative sources or consider saving seeds from your plants.
4. Personal Preferences and Goals: Your personal preferences and gardening goals should significantly influence your seed and variety selection. Consider factors such as your gardening experience, time commitment, space limitations, and aesthetic preferences. Choose seeds and varieties that align with your objectives if you have specific goals like creating a pollinator-friendly garden, growing a specific heirloom variety, or experimenting with new and unique plants.
5. Environmental Considerations: It's important to be mindful of environmental factors when choosing seeds and varieties. Opting for plants known to be drought-tolerant, low maintenance, or require fewer chemical inputs can contribute to water conservation, reduce the use of pesticides or fertilizers, and promote sustainable gardening practices. Native plant varieties

can also support local wildlife and contribute to ecological balance.
6. Experimentation and Learning: Gardening is a continuous learning process, and experimenting with different seeds and varieties can be an exciting part of the journey. Don't be afraid to try new and unfamiliar plants or explore unique heirloom varieties. Keep a gardening journal to document your experiences and observations, which can help you make better choices in the future and refine your gardening practices.

Remember, choosing the right seeds and varieties is not a one-size-fits-all approach. It's important to consider your specific circumstances, preferences, and goals when selecting. By taking the time to research, gather information, and make thoughtful choices, you can set yourself up for a rewarding and successful gardening experience.

Starting seeds indoors and outdoors

Starting seeds indoors and outdoors refers to germinating and growing plants from seeds in different environments. Each method has advantages and considerations, depending on factors such as the type of plant, climate, available space, and desired outcomes.
1. Starting Seeds Indoors: Indoor seed starting involves germinating seeds in a controlled

environment, typically within the confines of a home, greenhouse, or designated indoor growing space. Here are the key steps:

a. Seed selection: Choose high-quality seeds suitable for indoor cultivation. b. Containers and soil: Select appropriate containers such as trays, pots, or seedling cells. Use a sterile seed-starting mix or a light potting soil to promote healthy root development. c. Sowing seeds: Follow the instructions on the seed packet for the recommended depth and spacing. Typically, seeds are placed on the soil surface and lightly covered. d. Light and temperature: Provide adequate light by placing seedlings near a south-facing window or using artificial grow lights. Maintain a temperature suitable for seed germination and growth. e. Watering and care: Keep the soil consistently moist but not overly saturated. Avoid overwatering, as it can lead to damping-off or root rot. f. Transplanting: Once seedlings develop several true leaves, they can be transplanted into larger containers or hardened off and prepared for outdoor planting.

Benefits of starting seeds indoors include the ability to control growing conditions, start plants earlier in the season, extend the growing season, and protect young seedlings from pests and adverse weather conditions.

1. Starting Seeds Outdoors: Outdoor seed starting involves directly sowing seeds into the ground or containers outside. This

method is suitable for hardy plants that can withstand outdoor conditions or when indoor space is limited. Here are the key steps:

a. Soil preparation: Prepare the soil by removing weeds, loosening it, and adding organic matter if necessary. b. Sowing seeds: Follow the seed packet instructions for the appropriate depth and spacing. Plant the seeds directly into the prepared soil or containers. c. Watering and care: Keep the soil consistently moist during germination and early growth stages. Use a gentle watering method to avoid dislodging the seeds. d. Protection: Protect the seeds and seedlings from pests, birds, and extreme weather conditions as needed. e. Thinning: Once the seedlings emerge and develop their first true leaves, thin them to ensure proper spacing and optimal growth.

Starting seeds outdoors allows plants to acclimate to natural light and temperature variations from the beginning. It simplifies the transplanting process since the plants are already in their intended growing location. However, it may have limitations regarding the growing season, especially in colder climates.

Indoor Seed Starting:

1. Light source: Adequate lighting is crucial for indoor seed starting, especially if you don't have sufficient natural light. Consider using fluorescent or LED grow lights to provide the

necessary light spectrum for healthy seedling development.
2. Temperature control: Indoor environments usually provide more control over temperature than outdoor conditions. Most seeds germinate best within a specific temperature range. You can use a heating mat or adjustable thermostat to maintain optimal temperatures for germination.
3. Transplanting considerations: When transplanting seedlings are started indoors, it's important to harden them off gradually. Hardening off involves gradually exposing the seedlings to outdoor conditions over some time. This process helps the plants adjust to temperature fluctuations, wind, and direct sunlight, reducing the risk of transplant shock.

Outdoor Seed Starting:
1. Timing: It's crucial to consider the last frost date in your area when starting seeds outdoors. Some seeds are more cold-tolerant and can be sown earlier in the season, while others require warmer temperatures. Consult seed packets or gardening references to determine the appropriate time for outdoor sowing.
2. Protection from pests and elements: Outdoor-sown seeds are more vulnerable to pests, birds, and adverse weather conditions. To protect your seeds and

seedlings, you can use barriers like row covers, netting, or cloches. Regularly monitoring and promptly addressing any pest or disease issues are essential for successful outdoor seed starting.
3. Succession planting: With outdoor seed starting, you can practice succession planting by sowing new seeds at regular intervals. This ensures a continuous harvest throughout the growing season by staggering the maturity of the plants.
4. Direct sowing vs seedling transplanting: Some plants, such as root vegetables or large-seeded plants, prefer to be directly sown outdoors rather than starting indoors. Examples include carrots, radishes, beans, and corn. These plants have sensitive roots, making transplanting challenging, so they are typically sown directly into the garden soil.

Remember, the specific requirements and techniques for starting seeds indoors and outdoors can vary depending on the plant species and your specific growing conditions. Always refer to seed packets, gardening references, and local expertise for the best practices tailored to your situation. Happy gardening!

Transplanting seedlings for optimal growth
Transplanting seedlings refers to moving young plants from their initial germination or seedling

trays to larger containers or directly into the ground, allowing them to continue growing in a more suitable environment for their long-term development. This practice is commonly employed in gardening, horticulture, and commercial agriculture to promote optimal growth and ensure healthier, more robust plants. Here is an explanation of transplanting seedlings and its benefits for optimal growth:

1. Timing: Transplanting seedlings is typically done when they have developed a few sets of true leaves and have outgrown their initial containers or germination trays. At this stage, the seedlings are still young and adaptable, making it easier for them to adjust to their new growing conditions.
2. Larger Space: Moving seedlings to larger containers or planting them directly into the ground provides them with more space for root development. This increased root space allows for better nutrient uptake, water retention, and overall plant stability.
3. Nutrient Availability: Transplanting seedlings into fresh soil or potting mix ensures a steady supply of nutrients. The initial germination mix or tray soil may have limited nutrients, which can eventually deplete as the seedlings grow. By transplanting, you can provide the plants with a nutrient-rich medium that supports healthy growth.

4. Reduced Competition: When seedlings are initially sown in trays or close together, they compete for resources like light, water, and nutrients. Transplanting allows for adequate spacing between plants, reducing competition and enabling each seedling to receive the necessary resources for optimal growth.
5. Environmental Adaptation: Transplanting seedlings helps them acclimate to different environmental conditions gradually. For example, if seedlings are initially started indoors or in a greenhouse, transplanting them outdoors exposes them to natural sunlight, wind, and temperature fluctuations. This gradual transition strengthens the plants, making them better equipped to withstand outdoor conditions.
6. Disease and Pest Control: Transplanting seedlings can help minimize the risk of disease and pest infestation. Seedlings started indoors or in protected environments are more vulnerable to certain diseases and pests. By transplanting them, you can reduce the buildup of pathogens and pests, promoting healthier growth.
7. Long-Term Growth Potential: Properly transplanted seedlings have a higher chance of reaching their full growth potential. With ample space, nutrients, and reduced

competition, they can establish stronger root systems, develop sturdy stems, and produce larger foliage or fruits. This sets the stage for healthier, more productive plants in the long run.

To ensure successful transplantation, it is essential to handle the seedlings with care, avoid damaging the roots, and provide appropriate water and light conditions after transplanting. Additionally, gradually introducing seedlings to their new environment through a process called hardening off can enhance their chances of adapting well and thriving in their new location.

1. Transplant Shock: When seedlings are moved to a new environment, they may experience transplant shock. This is a temporary setback where the plants may exhibit wilting, yellowing of leaves, or stunted growth. To minimize transplant shock, it is crucial to handle the seedlings gently, avoid disturbing the roots excessively, and provide appropriate care and environmental conditions after transplanting.
2. Plant Spacing: Proper plant spacing is important for optimal growth. When transplanting, consider the recommended spacing requirements for the specific plant species. Providing adequate space between plants allows for better air circulation, reduces the risk of disease transmission, and

prevents overcrowding that can lead to competition for resources.
3. Watering Techniques: After transplanting, it is important to water the seedlings properly. Watering should be done gently and evenly to settle the soil around the roots and avoid excessive compaction. Be mindful not to overwater or underwater the seedlings, as both can hinder their growth. Monitoring the moisture level in the soil and adjusting watering accordingly is essential.
4. Fertilization: While transplanting seedlings into fresh soil or potting mix provides initial nutrients, additional fertilization may be necessary for optimal growth. Depending on the plant's nutritional requirements, you may need to supplement with organic or synthetic fertilizers. However, following the recommended dosage and application instructions is important to prevent fertilizer burn or nutrient imbalances.
5. Hardening Off: Before transplanting seedlings from indoor or protected environments to the outdoors, it is crucial to gradually expose them to outdoor conditions. This process is called hardening off and involves gradually increasing the amount of time the seedlings spend outside over several days or weeks. Hardening off helps the plants adjust to the temperature,

wind, and sunlight changes, reducing the likelihood of transplant shock.
6. Transplanting Techniques: When transplanting seedlings, it's important to handle them carefully and minimize root damage. Gently loosen the soil around the seedling's roots and lift them from the container or tray while holding onto the leaves, avoiding pulling them up by the stem. Place the seedling into the prepared hole or container, ensuring the roots are well-covered with soil or growing medium.
7. Mulching: Applying a layer of organic mulch around transplanted seedlings can provide several benefits. Mulch helps to retain soil moisture, suppress weed growth, regulate soil temperature, and prevent soil erosion. These factors contribute to healthier and more vigorous plant growth.

Remember that the specific transplanting techniques and practices may vary depending on the type of plant, its growth requirements, and the climate conditions in your region. It's always recommended to consult plant-specific guidelines or seek advice from experienced gardeners or horticulturists for the best results.

Chapter 5: Cultivation Techniques for Each Season

Cultivation techniques for each season refer to the specific agricultural practices and strategies employed during different seasons to maximize crop production and ensure successful plant growth. These techniques consider the unique environmental conditions, temperature variations, precipitation levels, and day length associated with each season. Here's an overview of cultivation techniques commonly used for each season:

1. Spring:
   - Soil preparation: Begin by clearing the field of debris and weeds. Loosen the soil using a tiller or hand tools to improve aeration and drainage.
   - Sowing and transplanting: Start planting cool-season crops like lettuce, spinach, peas, and carrots. Consider using row covers or cloches to protect tender seedlings from late frosts.
   - Irrigation: Monitor soil moisture and water as needed to support germination and early growth. Pay attention to weather patterns to avoid overwatering during periods of heavy rainfall.

- Weed control: Regularly remove weeds to prevent competition for nutrients and sunlight.
- Pest management: Keep an eye out for early signs of pests and diseases. Consider using organic pest control methods if necessary.

2. Summer:

- Water management: As temperatures rise, plants require increased water supply. Irrigate deeply and less frequently to encourage deep-root growth.
- Mulching: Apply organic mulch around plants to conserve soil moisture, suppress weed growth, and regulate soil temperature.
- Fertilization: Apply balanced fertilizers to support plant growth. Follow the recommended application rates and timings.
- Pollination: Support pollinators by planting flowers and providing suitable habitats. This is crucial for fruit set and crop yield.
- Shade and protection: Install shade cloths or shade structures to protect heat-sensitive plants from excessive sunlight and heat stress.
- Pest control: Regularly monitor for pests and apply appropriate measures such as insecticides or biological controls.

- Fall:
- Harvesting: Collect mature crops before the first frost or as indicated by the crop's maturity stage.
- Cover cropping: Sow cover crops like winter rye or clover to prevent soil erosion, improve soil fertility, and suppress weeds during the dormant season.
- Soil enrichment: Incorporate organic matter into the soil to enhance its structure and nutrient content.
- Pest and disease prevention: Clean up plant debris to reduce the risk of overwintering pests and diseases.
- Irrigation adjustment: Adjust irrigation schedules based on changing weather patterns and decreasing water requirements.

Winter:
- Crop rotation planning: Use the winter season to plan crop rotations for the following year, considering the nutrient needs of different crops and pest management strategies.
- Soil testing: Collect soil samples and send them for testing to determine nutrient deficiencies and pH levels.

- Equipment maintenance: Service and maintain farm machinery and equipment during the off-season to ensure they are ready for the next growing season.
- Greenhouse production: Utilize greenhouses or indoor growing spaces for winter cultivation of cold-tolerant crops.
- Cold protection: Employ row covers, tunnels, or other protective measures to shield crops from freezing temperatures.
- Remember, cultivation techniques can vary based on climate, region, and specific crops grown. It's always recommended to consult local agricultural extension services or experienced farmers for tailored advice based on your specific circumstances.

Here are some additional cultivation techniques for each season:

Spring:

- Crop rotation: Rotate crops each season to avoid depleting soil nutrients and minimize the risk of pests and diseases.
- Pruning and training: Trim and train fruit trees and vines to promote healthy growth and maximize yield.

- Soil amendment: Add compost or well-rotted manure to enrich the soil with organic matter and improve its fertility.
- Pest monitoring: Regularly inspect plants for signs of pests and employ integrated pest management (IPM) strategies to minimize damage.

Summer:

- Thinning and pruning: Thin out crowded plantings to allow proper air circulation and light penetration, reducing the risk of diseases.
- Water conservation: Use drip irrigation or water-efficient methods to minimize water usage and prevent water stress.
- Fruit thinning: Remove excess fruit from fruit trees to ensure better fruit quality and prevent branches from breaking under heavy loads.
- Trellising and support: Install trellises, cages, or stakes to support vining or tall plants, such as tomatoes or cucumbers.
- Harvesting at the right time: Regularly harvest ripe crops to maintain productivity and encourage continuous production.

Fall:

- Cold frame gardening: Utilize cold frames or hoop houses to extend the growing season for cool-season crops.
- Soil protection: Cover bare soil with straw or cover crops to prevent erosion and maintain soil structure.
- Fall cover cropping: Sow cover crops like legumes or winter wheat to fix nitrogen, suppress weeds, and improve soil fertility.
- Garden cleanup: Remove and dispose of diseased plants to prevent the overwintering of pests and diseases.
- Bulb planting: Plant spring-flowering bulbs, such as tulips or daffodils, in the fall for beautiful blooms the following year.

Winter:

- Indoor gardening: Grow herbs, micro greens, or dwarf varieties of vegetables indoors using containers and supplemental lighting.
- Seed selection and ordering: Research and select the seeds you'll need for the upcoming growing season and place orders in advance.
- Crop planning: Develop a detailed crop plan for the next growing season, including seed starting dates, succession planting, and crop rotations.
- Soil testing and amendment: Test the soil for nutrient levels and pH, and amend

accordingly to ensure optimal growing conditions.
- Education and learning: Use the winter months to attend agricultural workshops, conferences, or online courses to expand your knowledge and skills.
- These techniques provide a broad overview, but it's essential to adapt them to your specific climate, soil conditions, and crop choices. Always stay informed about local agricultural practices and seek guidance from experienced growers in your area.

Spring gardening: preparing for the growing season

Spring gardening is an exciting time for gardeners as it marks the beginning of the growing season. It is a crucial period when you need to prepare your garden to ensure healthy plant growth and maximize your harvest later in the year. Here are some essential steps to take when preparing for the growing season:

1. Clean and tidy up: Start by clearing away any debris, fallen leaves, and weeds accumulated over the winter. This will help prevent pests and

diseases from harbouring in your garden and provide a clean slate for new growth.

2. Soil preparation: Assess the quality of your soil. Test its pH level and nutrient content to determine if any amendments are necessary. Add organic matter, such as compost or well-rotted manure, to improve soil structure, drainage, and fertility. Loosen the soil with a garden fork or tiller to allow roots to penetrate easily.

3. Plan your garden layout: Decide which plants you want to grow and where to plant them. Consider factors like sunlight requirements, plant height, and compatibility between different species. This step helps optimize space, prevent overcrowding, and promotes healthy plant growth.

4. Start seedlings indoors: If you're growing plants from seeds, start them indoors several weeks before the last frost date in your area. Use seed trays or containers filled with a quality seed-starting mix. Ensure adequate light, warmth, and moisture for germination and early growth.

5. Prune and trim: Check your existing plants for dead or damaged branches. Prune them back to stimulate new growth and maintain plant health. Additionally, trim overgrown shrubs or trees to maintain their shape and size.

6.   Prepare for pests: Take preventive measures against common garden pests. Install physical barriers like fences or netting to protect your plants from animals. Consider using organic pest control methods or companion planting to deter insects naturally.

7.   Provide support structures: Some plants, such as tomatoes, cucumbers, or climbing vines, require support structures like trellises, stakes, or cages. Install these structures before planting to prevent root damage later on.

8.   Check and repair garden tools: Inspect your gardening tools, including shovels, hoes, and pruning shears. Clean them thoroughly, sharpen the blades, and replace any damaged parts. Well-maintained tools will make your gardening tasks easier and more efficient.

9.   Mulching: Apply a layer of organic mulch, such as wood chips or straw, around your plants. Mulch helps conserve moisture, suppresses weed growth, regulates soil temperature, and adds nutrients to the soil as it breaks down.

10.   Watering and fertilizing: Ensure proper watering based on the specific needs of your plants. Provide enough moisture without overwatering. Consider using organic fertilizers to provide essential nutrients for healthy growth.

11. Compost maintenance: If you have a compost bin, check on its progress and turn the compost if needed. This helps accelerate decomposition and ensures you have rich, nutrient-dense compost to add to your garden beds.

12. Test irrigation systems: If you have an irrigation system in place, inspect it for leaks, clogs, or damaged components. Test the system to ensure it is functioning properly and make any necessary repairs or adjustments.

13. Weed control: Spring is a crucial time to control weeds before they take over your garden. Remove any existing weeds and apply a weed suppressant or mulch to prevent new weed growth. Regularly monitor your garden and promptly remove any weeds that sprout.

14. Check for plant diseases: Inspect your plants for signs of diseases such as spots, wilting, or discolouration. If you identify any infected plants, remove them to prevent the spread of disease to other plants. Consider using organic disease control methods if necessary.

15. Prepare for frost: In regions where late spring frosts are possible, take precautions to protect tender plants. Have frost blankets or row covers ready to cover your plants when needed.

Keep an eye on weather forecasts and take appropriate action to safeguard your plants.

16. Consider companion planting: Utilize companion planting techniques to maximize space and deter pests. Certain plants have natural affinities for each other and can enhance growth or repel harmful insects when planted together. Research companion planting combinations for your chosen crops.

17. Start a garden journal: Maintain a garden journal to keep track of planting dates, weather conditions, and observations about your garden. This information can be valuable for future planning and troubleshooting.

18. Create a pollinator-friendly garden: Welcome beneficial pollinators by planting flowers that attract bees, butterflies, and other pollinators. These pollinators play a vital role in the success of many fruiting plants and contribute to overall garden biodiversity.

19. Consider organic gardening practices: Explore organic gardening methods to minimize synthetic chemicals and promote a healthier garden ecosystem. Use organic fertilizers, pest control methods, and cultural practices like crop rotation and companion planting.

20. Stay vigilant and flexible: Gardening is an ongoing process, and conditions can change throughout the season. Monitor your garden regularly, observe plant growth, and address any issues promptly. Stay open to adjusting your plans and techniques based on the specific needs of your garden.

Remember, gardening is a journey, and each season provides new opportunities to learn and grow. Enjoy the process, stay connected with your garden, and savour the rewards of your efforts as your plants flourish throughout the growing season.

Summer gardening: managing heat and water requirements

Summer gardening can be a rewarding and enjoyable experience, but it also comes with challenges, particularly when managing the heat and water requirements of your plants. Here are some key considerations and strategies for successfully managing your garden during the hot summer months:

1. Watering:

- Adequate watering is crucial during the summer as plants lose more water through evaporation and transpiration. Check your plants' water requirements by observing the soil moisture level and the appearance of the plants.

- Water deeply and infrequently to encourage deep root growth. Shallow watering leads to shallow root systems, making plants more susceptible to heat stress.

- Water your garden early in the morning or late in the evening to minimize water loss through evaporation. Avoid watering during the hottest part of the day, as the water can evaporate quickly.

- Consider using drip irrigation or soaker hoses to deliver water directly to the roots, reducing water waste through evaporation and ensuring efficient water usage.

- Mulch your garden beds with a layer of organic mulch, such as straw or wood chips, to conserve moisture, suppress weed growth, and regulate soil temperature.

2. Soil and Plant Protection:

- Improve your soil's ability to retain moisture by adding organic matter, such as compost or well-rotted manure, which helps increase water-holding capacity.

- Apply a layer of mulch around your plants to insulate the soil, prevent moisture loss, and reduce weed competition.

- Consider using shade cloth or row covers to provide temporary shade for delicate plants during extreme heat waves. This can help reduce stress and prevent sunburn on leaves.

- Group plants with similar water needs together, creating microclimates in your garden and optimizing water usage.

3. Plant Selection:

- Choose heat-tolerant and drought-resistant plant varieties well-suited to your local climate. Native plants and succulents are often more adapted to hot and dry conditions.

- Consider using container gardening or raised beds, as they allow for better control over soil moisture and drainage.

- If you have a limited water supply or live in an arid region, consider xeriscaping, which involves landscaping with plants that require minimal water once established.

4. Monitoring and Maintenance:

- Regularly monitor your garden for signs of heat stress, such as wilting, yellowing leaves, or drooping. Adjust your watering schedule accordingly.

- Check for pests and diseases, as they tend to thrive in hot and dry conditions. Maintain good garden hygiene and promptly address any issues to prevent further damage.

- Provide adequate airflow by spacing plants appropriately to reduce the risk of diseases that thrive in humid conditions.

5. Water Conservation:

- Consider installing a rainwater harvesting system to collect and store rainwater for later use in your garden. This can help reduce your reliance on municipal water sources and conserve water during dry periods.

- Use a watering can or a targeted hose attachment to water specific plants directly at their base, minimizing water waste.

- Regularly check for leaks in irrigation systems, hoses, and faucets to prevent water loss and ensure efficient water usage.

6. Proper Plant Care:

- Regularly inspect your plants for signs of pests and diseases, as these can weaken the plants and make them more susceptible to heat stress. Promptly address any issues through appropriate pest control and disease management techniques.

- Prune your plants selectively to remove dead or damaged foliage, improving air circulation and reducing the overall stress on the plant.

- Avoid fertilizing your plants during periods of extreme heat, as it can lead to salt burn and further stress the plants. Instead, focus on providing adequate water and maintaining overall plant health.

7. Shade Management:

- Use shade structures, such as umbrellas or shade sails, to provide temporary shade for potted plants or sensitive vegetables during the hottest parts of the day.

- Consider planting taller plants or using trellises to create natural shade for smaller, delicate plants.

- Avoid planting heat-sensitive plants in areas that receive intense, direct sunlight for prolonged periods. Instead, choose locations with partial shade or use shade cloth to filter sunlight.

8. Harvesting and Timing:

- Harvest fruits and vegetables early in the morning when they are cooler and retain more moisture.

- Plan your gardening activities and maintenance tasks for cooler parts of the day, such as mornings or evenings, to minimize stress on both you and the plants.

Remember, gardening practices can vary depending on your specific climate, soil conditions, and the types of plants you are growing. It's essential to observe and respond to your garden's needs accordingly. Regular monitoring, proper watering techniques, and adjusting your gardening practices as necessary will go a long way in ensuring the success of your summer garden.

Fall gardening: extending the harvest and preparing for winter

Fall gardening refers to the practice of continuing to grow and harvest crops during the autumn season and taking steps to prepare your garden for the upcoming winter. Extending the harvest and preparing for winter can maximize your garden's productivity and ensure its health for the following year.

Extending the Harvest:

1. Planting Fall Crops: Many vegetables and herbs can be planted in late summer or early fall

for a late-season harvest. Examples include leafy greens like lettuce, spinach, and kale, as well as root crops like carrots, radishes, and beets. These crops can withstand cooler temperatures and provide fresh produce well into the fall.

2. Protecting from Frost: As temperatures drop, protecting your plants from frost becomes crucial. Covering plants with frost blankets, row covers, or even cold frames can help create a barrier against frost and extend the growing season. Be sure to remove coverings during the day to allow sunlight and airflow.

3. Harvesting and Storing: Regularly harvest mature crops before the first frost. Pick vegetables at their peak ripeness and store them properly. Some vegetables, like pumpkins and winter squashes, can be stored for months if kept in a cool, dry place. Others, such as tomatoes, can be ripened indoors after picking.

Preparing for Winter:

1. Cleaning and Clearing: Remove any spent plants, weeds, and debris from your garden beds. This practice helps prevent the spread of diseases and pests. Clearing the garden also makes preparing the soil for the next growing season easier.

2. Soil Enrichment: Fall is an excellent time to amend the soil with organic matter. Add compost, well-rotted manure, or other soil amendments to replenish nutrients and improve soil structure. Turn the soil or use a garden fork to incorporate the amendments evenly.

3. Mulching: Applying a layer of organic mulch, such as straw or wood chips, over your garden beds helps insulate the soil and prevent weed growth. Mulching also conserves moisture and protects the soil from erosion during winter rains.

4. Protecting Perennials: If you have perennial plants in your garden, protect them from freezing temperatures by adding a layer of mulch around the base. This helps insulate the roots and prevents heaving caused by freezing and thawing cycles.

5. Tool Maintenance: Before winter sets in, clean and properly store your gardening tools. Remove any dirt, rust, or plant residue, and consider oiling metal parts to prevent corrosion. This maintenance ensures that your tools will be ready for use when the next gardening season arrives.

Here are some additional tips and techniques for fall gardening:

1. Succession Planting: As you harvest your summer crops, fill those empty spaces with quick-growing fall vegetables. Planting successions of fast-maturing crops like radishes, baby salad greens, and turnips ensures a continuous harvest throughout the fall.

2. Season Extension Structures: To protect your crops from cold temperatures, consider using season extension structures like cold frames, hoop houses, or greenhouses. These structures provide additional insulation and create a microclimate that allows you to grow more tender crops well into the winter.

3. Cover Crops: Planting cover crops, also known as green manure, is an excellent way to improve soil fertility and prevent erosion during winter. Cover crops like winter rye, clover, or field peas can be sown in the fall, and they will protect the soil, suppress weeds, and add organic matter when tilled under in the spring.

4. Pest and Disease Management: Fall is a good time to clean up your garden to reduce overwintering pests and diseases. Remove any diseased or pest-infested plants and dispose of them properly. This practice helps break the lifecycle of pests and reduces the likelihood of future infestations.

5. Watering and Irrigation: While the days may be cooler in the fall, it's essential to keep watering your plants as needed. Drier autumn weather and cool winds can quickly dehydrate plants, so monitor soil moisture and provide supplemental watering when necessary.

6. Harvesting and Seed Saving: As you harvest your fall crops, consider saving seeds from your best-performing plants. Properly dried and stored seeds can be used for next year's garden, saving you money and preserving desirable traits.

7. Garden Planning: Use the fall season to reflect on your garden's performance and make plans for the next year. Take note of which crops did well and which ones struggled. Consider rotating your crops to prevent pest and disease buildup and plan any changes or expansions for the coming growing season.

Remember to adjust your gardening practices based on your specific climate and region. Fall gardening can vary depending on your location, so it's always beneficial to consult with local gardening resources or experienced gardeners for tailored advice.

Winter gardening: strategies for cold-weather gardening

Winter gardening refers to the practice of growing plants during the colder months of the year when the temperatures drop, and the growing conditions become challenging. It requires specific strategies and techniques to protect plants from frost, ensure proper insulation, and provide them with the conditions for growth. Here are some strategies for cold-weather gardening:

1. Selecting appropriate plants: Choose cold-hardy plant varieties that can tolerate freezing temperatures and thrive in colder climates. Look for plants labelled as "winter-hardy," "frost-tolerant," or "cold-resistant." Examples include kale, cabbage, Brussels sprouts, winter lettuce, spinach, and certain herbs.

2. Extending the growing season: Start your winter garden early by sowing seeds indoors or in a greenhouse before the first frost. This allows plants to develop and establish themselves before transplanting them outdoors. Additionally, you can use techniques like row covers, cold frames, or cloches to protect plants from frost and extend the growing season.

3. Providing insulation: Insulate the soil by applying a thick layer of mulch around plants. This helps to regulate soil temperature, retain moisture, and protect the roots from extreme cold. Suitable mulching materials include straw, leaves, pine needles, or compost.

4. Using protective coverings: In regions with severe winters, protective coverings are essential. Floating row covers made of lightweight fabric can be draped over plants to create a barrier against cold winds and frost. Additionally, cold frames or mini-greenhouses can provide extra protection for delicate plants.

5. Cold-tolerant crops and varieties: Choose crops specifically adapted to withstand cold temperatures. Some plants can tolerate freezing temperatures and continue to produce even in winter. Examples include winter varieties of carrots, beets, turnips, and certain types of radishes.

6. Watering considerations: Watering requirements differ in winter gardening. While the plants still need moisture, they require less water compared to warmer months. Avoid overwatering, as excessive moisture can lead to freezing damage. Water plants during the

warmest part of the day to prevent freezing at night.

7. Crop rotation and succession planting: Practice crop rotation to prevent the buildup of pests and diseases. Additionally, consider succession planting to maximize the use of space and ensure a continuous harvest throughout the winter. Planting new seeds or seedlings at intervals allows for a staggered harvest.

8. Utilizing heat sources: In extremely cold climates, providing additional heat sources can protect plants from freezing. This can include using frost blankets, heat lamps, or even small heaters inside cold frames or greenhouses to maintain a suitable temperature for plant growth.

9. Windbreaks: Strong winds can significantly affect plants during the winter. Consider creating windbreaks using structures like fences, hedges, or temporary barriers made of burlap or plastic. Windbreaks help reduce wind velocity, protecting plants from desiccation and damage.

10. Cold-tolerant herbs: Grow herbs that can withstand colder temperatures, such as rosemary, thyme, sage, and chives. These herbs can add flavour to your winter dishes and continue to thrive even in chilly conditions.

11. Cold-resistant containers: If you're gardening in containers, choose containers made of materials that can withstand freezing temperatures, such as plastic or fibreglass. Avoid using terracotta or ceramic pots, as they can crack when exposed to freezing and thawing cycles.

12. Watering techniques: During winter, water evaporates more slowly, and plants may not need frequent watering. Adjust your watering schedule according to the moisture requirements of your plants and the weather conditions. Watering deeply but infrequently can help prevent waterlogged soil and minimize the risk of freezing.

13. Indoor gardening: If you have limited outdoor space or live in an extremely cold climate, consider setting up an indoor garden. You can grow a variety of herbs, microgreens, and even dwarf fruit trees using grow lights or by placing them near a south-facing window that receives ample sunlight.

14. Soil preparation: Before winter, ensure that your soil is well-drained and enriched with organic matter. This improves soil structure, provides essential nutrients, and helps retain moisture. Amend the soil with compost or well-rotted manure to enhance its fertility and water-holding capacity.

15. Cold frame maintenance: If you're using a cold frame, regularly monitor the temperature inside to ensure it doesn't get too hot or too cold. Ventilation is crucial to prevent overheating, especially on sunny days. Open the lids or doors during the day and close them at night to maintain an optimal temperature.

16. Pest management: Even in winter, pests can be a concern. Monitor your plants regularly for signs of pest damage and take appropriate measures to control them. Inspect your plants carefully before bringing them indoors from an outdoor winter garden to avoid introducing pests into your home.

17. Harvesting techniques: Learn the ideal time to harvest winter crops. Some vegetables, such as kale and Brussels sprouts, taste sweeter after being exposed to frost. Harvest them when they are at their peak flavour. Additionally, harvest root crops like carrots and beets as needed, leaving the rest in the ground until you're ready to use them.

By implementing these additional strategies, you can further enhance your winter gardening experience and maximize the productivity of your cold-weather garden.

Chapter 6: Pest and Disease Management

Pest and disease management is a crucial aspect of agriculture and gardening that involves preventing, detecting, and controlling pests and diseases that can negatively impact plants, crops, and ecosystems. Pests refer to any organisms, such as insects, rodents, birds, or weeds, that cause harm or damage to plants. On the other hand, diseases are caused by microorganisms such as bacteria, fungi, viruses, or nematodes.

Effective pest and disease management aims to minimize the damage caused by these organisms and ensure the health and productivity of plants. It involves implementing various strategies and practices to prevent infestations, identify problems early, and apply appropriate control measures.

Here are some key components of pest and disease management:

1. Prevention: Prevention is The best pest and disease management approach. This involves maintaining plant health through proper cultivation practices, such as providing adequate nutrition, irrigation, and optimal growing conditions. It also includes selecting disease-

resistant or pest-tolerant plant varieties and using healthy seeds or seedlings.

2.   Monitoring: Regular monitoring of plants is essential to detect the presence of pests or diseases at an early stage. This can be done through visual inspection, trapping, or various monitoring tools. Monitoring helps identify the type and severity of the problem and allows for timely intervention.

3.   Cultural practices: Cultural practices refer to a range of techniques that create unfavourable conditions for pests and diseases or improve plant resistance. Examples include crop rotation, intercropping, proper spacing, pruning, and removing diseased plant material. These practices disrupt the life cycle of pests, reduce the buildup of pathogens, and promote plant vigour.

4.   Biological control: Biological control involves using natural enemies of pests, such as predators, parasitoids, or pathogens, to suppress pest populations. This approach is environmentally friendly and can provide long-term pest control. For example, ladybugs can be released to control aphids, or certain fungi can be applied to control plant diseases.

5.   Chemical control: When other methods are insufficient, chemical control measures can be used. Pesticides are chemicals designed to kill or

inhibit the growth of pests. However, their use should be reasonable and by recommended guidelines to minimize environmental and human health risks. Integrated Pest Management (IPM) approaches promote the targeted and selective use of pesticides as a last resort.

6. Education and awareness: Knowledge and awareness about pest and disease management techniques are crucial for effective implementation. Farmers, gardeners, and agricultural professionals should stay updated with the latest information, research findings, and best practices to make informed decisions and take appropriate actions.

7. Integrated Pest Management (IPM): IPM is a comprehensive approach combining multiple strategies to effectively manage pests and diseases. It emphasizes using a combination of cultural, biological, and chemical control methods tailored to the specific pest or disease problem. IPM focuses on minimizing economic, environmental, and health risks while maintaining pest populations at tolerable levels.

8. Quarantine and biosecurity: Quarantine measures involve isolating and inspecting plants, seeds, or other agricultural products to prevent the introduction and spread of pests and diseases.

Biosecurity practices, such as controlled access, hygiene protocols, and proper sanitation, are implemented to protect plants from external sources of infestation and to prevent the spread of diseases within a farm or garden.

9. Resistant plant varieties: Plant breeding programs aim to develop crop varieties with natural resistance or tolerance to specific pests and diseases. By selecting and planting resistant varieties, farmers and gardeners can reduce their reliance on pesticides and minimize damage caused by pests and diseases.

10. Traps and monitoring devices: Traps and monitoring devices are used to attract and capture pests or detect their presence. These tools can be used to monitor population levels, assess the effectiveness of control measures, and make informed decisions on pest management strategies.

11. Forecasting and early warning systems: Some pests and diseases have specific environmental requirements for development and spread. Forecasting models and early warning systems use weather data, biological indicators, and other factors to predict and alert farmers or gardeners about potential pest and disease outbreaks. This allows for proactive measures to

be taken, such as timely application of control methods.

12. Education and training: Promoting knowledge and training on pest and disease management practices is essential. This includes educating farmers, gardeners, and agricultural professionals on identifying pests and diseases, their life cycles, and suitable management techniques. Training programs can also focus on promoting sustainable and environmentally friendly approaches.

13. Record-keeping and analysis: Keeping records of pest and disease occurrences, control measures applied, and their effectiveness is crucial for improving management strategies over time. Analyzing this data helps identify patterns, assess trends, and refine pest and disease management practices for future seasons.

By employing these various strategies and staying vigilant, farmers, gardeners, and agricultural professionals can effectively manage pests and diseases, minimize crop losses, and promote sustainable agricultural practices.

Identifying common garden pests and diseases

Identifying common garden pests and diseases is an essential skill for gardeners and plant enthusiasts. Pests and diseases can cause significant damage to plants, leading to reduced yields, stunted growth, or even the death of the plant if left untreated. By recognizing the signs and symptoms of common pests and diseases, gardeners can take appropriate measures to control and prevent further damage.

Here are some key steps to identify common garden pests and diseases:

1. Observation: Regularly inspect your plants and pay attention to any changes in their appearance. Look for signs of damage, discolouration, wilting, holes in leaves, or unusual growth patterns. It's important to note that not all pests or diseases leave visible signs, so observing the behaviour of plants can also provide clues.

2. Research: Familiarize yourself with common pests and diseases that are prevalent in your region or known to affect the specific plants in your garden. Local gardening resources, books, websites, or agricultural extension offices can provide valuable information on common issues.

3. Visual cues: Pests and diseases often have distinct visual cues associated with them. Look for specific patterns or characteristics that can help you narrow down the possible causes. For example, spider mites leave fine webbing on

plants, while aphids are often found clustered on the undersides of leaves.

4. Signs of damage: Different pests and diseases cause different plant damage. Some chew on leaves, causing irregular holes or notches, while others suck sap, causing wilting, discolouration, or deformities. Examine the affected plant parts closely to identify the type of damage.

5. Symptoms: In addition to visible signs of damage, plants may exhibit symptoms such as yellowing leaves, stunted growth, leaf curling, or mould or fungal growth. These symptoms can provide further clues to the underlying issue.

6. Insect identification: If you suspect an insect pest, try to capture or collect a sample for closer examination. Use a magnifying glass or consult an insect identification guide to determine the specific pest species. This will help you select the appropriate treatment or control method.

7. Disease diagnosis: If you suspect a plant disease, take note of the symptoms and compare them to known diseases. Fungal, bacterial, and viral diseases often have distinct characteristics that can aid in diagnosis. Some diseases may require laboratory testing for accurate identification, so consulting with a plant

pathologist or agricultural expert may be necessary in some cases.

8. Seek help: If you're unsure about the identification or treatment of a pest or disease, don't hesitate to seek advice from local gardening experts, agricultural extension services, or plant clinics. They can provide professional guidance and recommend appropriate remedies or treatments.

By familiarizing yourself with common garden pests and diseases and practising regular observation, you'll become better equipped to identify and address issues promptly, thereby protecting your garden and promoting healthy plant growth.

Common Garden Pests:

1. Aphids: These small, soft-bodied insects feed on plant sap and can be found in large numbers on the undersides of leaves. They can cause distorted growth and transmit plant diseases.

2. Caterpillars: Various types of caterpillars, such as cabbage worms and tomato hornworms, can munch on leaves and damage crops. They often leave behind large holes or skeletonized leaves.

3. Snails and Slugs: These molluscs are notorious for eating plant foliage, leaving irregular holes and slime trails. They are more active during damp conditions.

4. Whiteflies: These tiny, white insects congregate on the undersides of leaves and suck plant sap. Their feeding can lead to yellowing leaves, stunted growth, and the transmission of plant viruses.

5. Spider Mites: These microscopic pests are difficult to see without magnification. They feed on plant sap and create tiny, web-like structures on leaves. Infested plants may show yellow speckling or stippling on the leaves.

Common Garden Diseases:

1. Powdery Mildew: This fungal disease appears as a white, powdery coating on leaves, stems, and flowers. It can cause stunted growth, yellowing, and premature leaf drop.

2. Black Spot: The black spot is a fungal disease that affects roses and other plants. It causes black spots to form on leaves, eventually turning yellow and dropping off.

3. Tomato Blight: Different types of blight affect tomatoes, such as early blight and late

blight. These diseases cause leaf spots, wilting, and fruit rot, often leading to significant crop loss.

4. Downy Mildew: Downy mildew affects various plants, including cucumbers, grapes, and lettuce. It causes yellow patches on the upper surface of leaves and fuzzy, purplish-grey growth on the undersides.

5. Root Rot: Root rot is a common problem caused by fungal pathogens that attack plant roots, leading to rotting, wilting, and overall decline. Overwatering and poorly drained soil can contribute to its development.

Remember that these are just a few examples, and numerous other pests and diseases can impact garden plants. It's important to research and learn about the specific pests and diseases that are prevalent in your region and those that affect the plants you are growing. This knowledge will help you in early detection and appropriate treatment or prevention measures.

Natural and organic pest control methods

Natural and organic pest control methods refer to using environmentally friendly and non-toxic techniques to manage and eliminate pests without relying on synthetic chemicals or harmful pesticides. These methods prioritize protecting human health, wildlife, and the overall ecosystem while effectively controlling pests.

Here are some commonly used natural and organic pest control methods:

1. Biological Control: This method involves introducing natural predators, parasites, or pathogens that naturally feed on or infect pests, effectively reducing their populations. For example, releasing ladybugs to control aphids or using nematodes to combat soil-borne pests.

2. Mechanical Control: This approach involves physically removing pests or using barriers to prevent their access. Examples include manually picking off pests, using traps or sticky tapes, or installing physical barriers like nets or fences.

3. Cultural Control: This method focuses on altering the environment or practices to discourage pests and promote healthy plant growth. Practices include crop rotation, companion planting (planting beneficial plants together), maintaining proper sanitation, and providing optimal conditions for plants to reduce susceptibility to pests.

4. Organic Pesticides: Organic pesticides derived from natural sources, such as plant extracts, essential oils, or naturally occurring minerals, can be used as alternatives to synthetic

chemical pesticides. These organic pesticides target specific pests while minimizing harm to beneficial organisms and the environment.

5. Insecticidal Soaps and Oils: Soaps and oils derived from plants, such as neem oil or insecticidal soaps, can be used to control pests. They work by suffocating or disrupting the pests' protective coatings, leading to their demise.

6. Physical Pest Barriers: Creating physical barriers, such as using row covers or mesh screens, helps prevent insects, birds, or other pests from reaching plants while allowing sunlight, water, and air to penetrate.

7. Integrated Pest Management (IPM): IPM combines multiple pest control strategies, including natural and organic methods, to manage pests effectively while minimizing environmental impact. It involves monitoring pests, identifying thresholds, and applying appropriate control methods at the right time.

8. Companion Planting: Certain plants have natural properties that repel pests or attract beneficial insects. By strategically planting these companion plants alongside susceptible crops, you can help deter pests. For example, marigolds are known to repel aphids, nematodes, and whiteflies.

9. Beneficial Insects: Introducing beneficial insects into the garden can help control pest populations. Ladybugs, lacewings, and praying mantises are beneficial insects that feed on pests like aphids, mites, and caterpillars.

10. Crop Rotation: Rotating crops annually can disrupt the life cycles of pests and reduce their buildup in the soil. Planting different crops in a specific sequence can help break the pest cycle and prevent their recurrence.

11. Traps and Barriers: Using traps and barriers is an effective way to control pests. Sticky traps can be placed to capture flying insects like fruit flies or gnats, while pheromone traps can be used to lure and trap specific pests. Additionally, physical barriers like copper tape around plant pots can deter slugs and snails.

12. Cultural Practices: Implementing good cultural practices can contribute to pest prevention. This includes proper watering and fertilization to promote plant health and resilience, timely pruning to remove infested plant parts, and regular garden cleanup to remove hiding places for pests.

13. Mulching: Mulching with organic materials like straw, wood chips, or compost can help suppress weed growth, retain moisture, and create

a barrier that hinders certain pests from reaching plants.

14. Handpicking: For small-scale infestations, physically removing pests by hand can be an effective control method. This is commonly done with larger insects like beetles or caterpillars.

15. Natural Repellents: Some natural substances have repellent properties against pests. For instance, garlic and chilli pepper sprays can deter insects and diatomaceous earth can be used to control crawling pests by damaging their exoskeletons.

It's important to note that while natural and organic pest control methods are generally safer and less harmful to the environment, they may not provide instant or complete eradication of pests. Regular monitoring, early detection, and consistent application of these methods may be necessary for long-term success.

Companion planting and beneficial insects

Companion planting and beneficial insects are two methods used in gardening and agriculture to promote healthy plant growth, increase crop yields, and reduce the need for pesticides.

Companion planting is the practice of planting different crops together nearby, taking advantage of the beneficial interactions they can have with each other. Certain plants have natural attributes that can repel pests, attract beneficial insects, or provide support and shade to neighbouring plants. By strategically combining compatible plants, gardeners can create a more balanced ecosystem in their gardens.

Here are some examples of companion planting strategies:

1. Pest control: Some plants produce natural chemicals or scents that repel specific pests. For instance, marigolds are known to deter nematodes, a type of soil-dwelling pest that can damage plant roots. Planting marigolds near susceptible crops can help protect them from these pests.

2. Attracting beneficial insects: Many insects benefit gardens as they prey on common pests. Planting flowers, such as lavender, daisies, or yarrow, can attract beneficial insects like ladybugs, lacewings, and parasitic wasps, which feed on aphids, caterpillars, and other garden pests.

3. Nitrogen fixation: Some plants can fix nitrogen from the air and make it available to other plants. Legumes, such as peas, beans, and

clover, have a symbiotic relationship with nitrogen-fixing bacteria in their roots. Planting legumes in or near vegetable beds can help improve soil fertility by increasing nitrogen levels.

4. Shade and support: Tall or vining plants can provide shade and support for other crops. For example, planting corn alongside beans allows the beans to climb the corn stalks, providing support while the corn benefits from the nitrogen-fixing properties of the beans.

Beneficial insects are organisms that play a crucial role in controlling pest populations by preying on or parasitizing them. By encouraging these insects to thrive in the garden, gardeners can reduce the need for chemical pesticides. Some common beneficial insects include ladybugs, lacewings, hoverflies, parasitic wasps, and praying mantises.

To attract beneficial insects to your garden, you can:

1. Provide habitat: Create diverse habitats in your garden by incorporating flowering plants, shrubs, and trees that offer shelter, nectar, and pollen sources for beneficial insects. Also, include water sources like birdbaths or shallow dishes with stones for them to drink from.

2. Avoid pesticides: Minimize or eliminate the use of pesticides, especially broad-spectrum ones

that can harm beneficial insects. If pest populations become problematic, consider using targeted or organic pest control methods that are less harmful to beneficial insects.

3. Plant for continuous bloom: Choose a variety of flowering plants that bloom at different times throughout the growing season. This ensures a continuous food source for beneficial insects, allowing them to establish and maintain populations in your garden.

By implementing companion planting and attracting beneficial insects, gardeners can create a more balanced and sustainable garden ecosystem. These methods promote natural pest control, reduce reliance on chemical interventions, and ultimately lead to healthier plants and higher crop yields.

1. Trap cropping: This technique involves planting a sacrificial crop that is particularly attractive to pests. By luring the pests away from the main crop, the trap crop can help protect the desired plants. For example, planting a patch of radishes or mustard greens to attract flea beetles away from vulnerable crops like eggplants or tomatoes.

2. Repellent plants: Certain plants have natural repellent properties that can deter pests. For

instance, planting strong-scented herbs like rosemary, sage, or thyme near susceptible plants can help repel insects. Similarly, aromatic plants like onions, garlic, or chives can deter pests due to their strong smell.

3. Polyculture: Polyculture refers to growing multiple crops together in the same area rather than monoculture (planting a single crop). This practice increases biodiversity and can confuse pests, making it harder for them to locate their preferred plants. It also helps utilize space more efficiently and reduces the risk of widespread crop failure due to a single pest or disease.

4. Companion planting in permaculture: Permaculture is an approach to gardening and agriculture that aims to mimic natural ecosystems and maximize sustainability. In permaculture systems, companion planting is often integrated with other elements such as trees, shrubs, and perennial plants to create a self-sustaining and resilient ecosystem. These systems can provide habitat for beneficial insects, improve soil health, conserve water, and reduce the overall maintenance required.

5. Beneficial insect attractants: In addition to flowers, there are other methods to attract beneficial insects. For example, providing suitable

nesting sites like small piles of twigs or hollow bamboo can attract solitary bees, which are important pollinators. Additionally, incorporating diverse plant species can attract a wider range of beneficial insects, as different species prefer different flowers and habitats.

6. Observation and experimentation: Companion planting and attracting beneficial insects can be dynamic. Observing and recording the interactions between plants and insects in your garden is important. Experiment with different combinations of companion plants and observe their effects on pests and beneficial insects. This can help you refine your approach and find the best strategies for your garden and climate.

While companion planting and attracting beneficial insects can be effective pest control methods, they may not eliminate all pest problems. It's important to maintain overall garden health by providing adequate water, proper nutrition, and good cultural practices to ensure the plants can resist pests and diseases to the best of their ability.

Chapter 7: Innovative Gardening Methods

Innovative gardening refers to new and creative approaches to cultivating plants, flowers, and vegetables. These methods often involve utilizing advanced technologies, sustainable practices, and unconventional techniques to improve gardening efficiency, productivity, and sustainability. Here are some examples of innovative gardening methods:

1. Vertical Gardening: This method involves growing plants vertically, using walls, trellises, or stacked containers. It maximizes space utilization and allows for growing a variety of plants in limited areas, such as urban environments.
2. Hydroponics: Hydroponic gardening involves growing plants without soil. Instead, plants are grown in nutrient-rich water solutions, allowing for precise control over nutrients, water, and light. Hydroponics uses less water, reduces the risk of pests and diseases, and enables year-round cultivation.
3. Aquaponics: Aquaponics combines aquaculture (fish farming) and hydroponics. It creates a symbiotic relationship where fish waste provides nutrients for plants, and the plants filter and purify the water for the fish. It is an efficient and sustainable

method that conserves resources and produces fish and vegetables.
4. Aeroponics: Aeroponics involves growing plants in an air or mist environment without soil or a growing medium. Plant roots are suspended in air, and nutrient-rich mist is periodically sprayed onto them. It allows for faster growth, reduces water usage, and requires minimal space.
5. Companion Planting: Companion planting is the practice of growing different plants together to benefit each other. For example, planting marigolds near vegetables can repel pests, or growing beans near corn provides natural nitrogen fixation, benefiting both plants.
6. Permaculture: Permaculture is an ecological design approach that aims to create sustainable, self-sufficient ecosystems. It involves designing landscapes that mimic natural patterns, promoting biodiversity, conserving water, and optimizing energy use. Permaculture gardens often incorporate food forests, composting, and natural pest control methods.
7. Smart Gardening: Smart gardening utilizes technologies like sensors, automation, and data analysis to optimize plant growth. It involves monitoring and controlling environmental factors such as light, temperature, humidity, and watering

through smartphone apps or intelligent systems. Smart gardening ensures precise and efficient resource utilization.

8. Rooftop Gardening: Rooftop gardens utilize unused rooftop spaces in urban areas for gardening. They help reduce the urban heat island effect, improve air quality, and provide insulation for buildings. Rooftop gardens often employ lightweight growing mediums, vertical structures, and efficient irrigation systems.

9. Green Roofs: Green roofs cover the surface of a building with vegetation, creating a living roof. They provide insulation, reduce stormwater runoff, absorb pollutants, and create habitats for wildlife. Green roofs can be used for growing various plants, including herbs, flowers, and even small trees.

10. Seed Bombs: Seed bombs are small balls made of clay, compost, and seeds. They are thrown or placed in specific areas to promote natural reforestation or the growth of wildflowers. Seed bombs can be an effective way to restore or beautify areas with low vegetation.

11. Microgreens and Sprouting: Microgreens are young vegetable greens harvested shortly after germination. They are packed with nutrients and are easy to grow indoors. Sprouting involves

germinating seeds and consuming young shoots. Both methods allow for quick and nutritious harvests in small spaces.
12. No-Dig Gardening: Also known as lasagna gardening or sheet mulching, this method involves layering organic materials such as cardboard, compost, straw, and leaves directly on the ground. The layers decompose over time, creating a fertile soil bed without the need for tilling or digging.
13. Community Gardens: Community gardens are shared spaces where individuals or groups come together to cultivate plants collectively. These gardens promote community engagement, food security, and knowledge exchange. They often include shared resources, educational programs, and social activities.
14. Robot-assisted Farming: Advancements in robotics have led to the development of robots designed to assist with gardening and farming tasks. These robots can perform activities like planting, weeding, and harvesting, reducing the need for manual labour and improving efficiency.
15. Biodynamic Farming: Biodynamic farming is an approach that integrates organic farming principles with holistic and spiritual perspectives. It emphasizes the interrelationships between soil, plants, animals, and the cosmos. Biodynamic

practices include using specific preparations, following lunar cycles, and creating self-sustaining ecosystems.
16. Seed Saving and Genetic Preservation: Seed saving involves collecting and storing seeds from open-pollinated plants to preserve their genetic diversity. This practice helps maintain heirloom and rare plant varieties and fosters seed sovereignty and resilience in agriculture.

These additional methods showcase the diverse range of innovative approaches to gardening and farming. They reflect the growing interest in sustainable practices, resource conservation, and the integration of technology and ecological principles into horticulture and agriculture.

Container gardening: maximizing space and portability

Container gardening is a method of growing plants in pots, containers, or other portable gardening vessels rather than directly in the ground. It offers several advantages, including maximizing space utilization and providing portability.

Maximizing Space: Container gardening is particularly useful in situations with limited space, such as in urban areas or small balconies. Using containers, you can use vertical space efficiently by stacking pots or utilizing hanging baskets. This allows you to grow various plants even in a small area.

Additionally, container gardening allows you to optimize the growing conditions for different plants. You can select containers of various sizes and shapes to accommodate plants with different root systems. For example, shallow pots work well for herbs, while deeper containers are suitable for vegetables like tomatoes or root crops like carrots. By tailoring the containers to the specific needs of each plant, you can maximize their growth potential.

Portability: One of the significant advantages of container gardening is the ability to move plants as needed. Containers can be easily relocated to maximize optimal sunlight, protect plants from harsh weather conditions, or create aesthetic arrangements. This mobility also allows you to bring your garden indoors during colder or inclement weather, extending the growing season.

Portability is particularly beneficial for renters or people living in temporary housing, as they can easily take their garden with them when they move. It also enables gardeners to experiment with different layouts or designs without making permanent changes to the landscape.

Another advantage of portability is the ability to control pests and diseases. If a plant becomes infested or infected, you can isolate it by moving the container away from other plants, reducing the risk of spreading the problem.

Getting Started with Container Gardening: To start container gardening, you will need appropriate containers, potting soil, plants or seeds, and access to sunlight and water. Choose containers with drainage holes to prevent waterlogging, and ensure they are large enough to accommodate the mature size of the plant.

Select plants suitable for container gardening, considering factors such as sunlight requirements, space limitations, and the container's size. Herbs, salad greens, flowers, and certain vegetables like peppers and lettuce are commonly grown in containers. Consider the specific needs of each plant, such as water requirements and preferred soil conditions.

When planting, use a high-quality potting mix that provides proper drainage and nutrients for the plants. Regularly monitor the moisture levels in the soil and adjust watering accordingly. Fertilize the plants as needed to ensure healthy growth.

In conclusion, container gardening is an excellent way to maximize space and portability in gardening. It allows you to grow plants in a confined area, adapt to different growing conditions, and easily move your garden as necessary. Whether you have limited space, want to enhance your living environment, or desire the flexibility of a portable garden, container gardening offers a practical and enjoyable solution.

Here are some additional tips and considerations for maximizing space and portability in container gardening:

1. Vertical Gardening: Take advantage of vertical space by using trellises, stakes, or other supports for vining plants such as tomatoes, cucumbers, or beans. This allows the plants to grow upward, saving horizontal space.
2. Companion Planting: Practice companion planting by combining plants with mutually beneficial relationships. For example, growing tall, sun-loving plants alongside smaller, shade-tolerant ones can optimize space and light utilization.
3. Succession Planting: To make the most of limited space, practice succession planting. As one crop finishes, replant the container with a new crop to ensure a continuous harvest throughout the growing season.
4. Dwarf and Compact Varieties: Choose dwarf or compact varieties of plants whenever possible. These varieties are specifically bred to grow well in containers, taking up less space while still producing a good yield.
5. Hanging Baskets and Window Boxes: Utilize hanging baskets and window boxes to grow trailing plants, herbs, or flowers. They add

visual interest and use vertical space, especially in areas with limited floor space.
6. Grouping and Stacking Containers: Cluster containers together, placing taller plants at the back and shorter ones in the front. This creates a visually appealing arrangement while maximizing space usage. You can also stack smaller containers on top of larger ones, creating a tiered effect.
7. Soil Conservation: Use a lightweight potting mix and consider adding perlite or vermiculite to improve drainage and reduce the weight of the containers. This makes it easier to move them when needed.
8. Mobility and Drainage: Place containers on casters or wheeled platforms to enhance portability. Ensure containers have proper drainage to prevent waterlogging and make them easier to transport.
9. Seasonal Rotation: Consider rotating your container plants based on the seasons. During the warmer months, place containers in areas with more sunlight, and during winter or extreme weather conditions, move them indoors or to more sheltered locations.
10. Watering and Fertilizing: Container plants require more frequent watering than plants in the ground since containers can dry out faster. Develop a watering schedule and monitor the moisture levels regularly.

Use a slow-release or liquid fertilizer to provide essential nutrients to the plants.
Remember to choose plants that are suitable for your climate and the specific conditions of your location. With careful planning, thoughtful selection of containers and plants, and proper care, you can create a thriving container garden that maximizes space, offers portability, and brings beauty and fresh produce to any setting.

Raised beds and vertical gardening: optimizing growing areas

Raised beds and vertical gardening are two techniques used in gardening to optimize growing areas and maximize productivity. Both methods are especially popular in urban or limited space environments where the available land for gardening is limited.

Raised beds involve creating a designated planting area that is elevated from the ground level. This is typically done by constructing a rectangular or square-shaped frame using materials such as wood, stone, or concrete. The bed is then filled with a mixture of soil, compost, and other organic matter to create a nutrient-rich growing environment.

There are several advantages to using raised beds:
1. Improved soil quality: By filling the raised bed with a custom soil mix, gardeners can ensure optimal soil conditions for plant growth. This is particularly beneficial in

areas with poor soil quality or heavy clay content.
2. Better drainage: Raised beds provide excellent drainage as they are elevated above the ground. This prevents waterlogging and ensures that plants' roots have access to oxygen, which is crucial for their health and growth.
3. Weed control: Raised beds help to minimize weed growth as they provide a physical barrier between the garden soil and surrounding weed seeds. This reduces the need for frequent weeding and allows plants to thrive without competition from unwanted plants.
4. Easy maintenance: Raised beds are easier to maintain since they can be designed at a height that reduces the strain on the gardener's back, making planting, watering, and harvesting more comfortable.

Vertical gardening, on the other hand, involves utilizing vertical space to grow plants. Instead of planting in traditional horizontal garden beds, plants are grown vertically using structures such as trellises, fences, or specially designed vertical gardening systems. Here's how vertical gardening optimizes growing areas:

1. Space efficiency: Vertical gardening allows you to grow plants vertically, utilizing the vertical space available. This is especially useful in small gardens or areas with limited

ground space. By going upward, you can increase the number of plants you can grow within a given area.
2. Improved sunlight exposure: Vertical gardening helps maximize sunlight exposure for plants. By growing vertically, plants can be positioned to receive more direct sunlight throughout the day, leading to better photosynthesis and healthier plant growth.
3. Aesthetically pleasing: Vertical gardens can add visual interest and beauty to your gardening space. They can transform bare walls or fences into vibrant green spaces, making them an appealing option for urban gardens or areas with limited ground space.
4. Better air circulation: When plants are grown vertically, there is increased air circulation around the foliage, reducing the risk of diseases and pests. This can result in healthier plants and less reliance on chemical interventions.

By combining raised beds and vertical gardening techniques, gardeners can optimize their growing areas even further. Raised beds provide a controlled and enriched soil environment, while vertical gardening utilizes the vertical space efficiently, allowing for an increased number of plants to be grown. Together, these methods can maximize productivity, improve aesthetics, and make gardening more accessible in various settings.

Raised Beds: 5. Extended growing season: Raised beds warm up more quickly in the spring compared to ground-level soil, allowing for earlier planting and an extended growing season. The elevated position of the beds helps them absorb more sunlight and retain heat, creating a microclimate that promotes plant growth.

1. Easy customization: Raised beds offer flexibility in terms of size and shape. Gardeners can customize the dimensions of the beds to suit their needs and preferences. They can also be built at a height that is comfortable for gardeners of all ages and physical abilities.
2. Pest control: Raised beds can help deter certain pests, such as burrowing animals or crawling insects, as the elevated structure creates a barrier. Additionally, it's easier to implement protective measures, such as installing netting or covers, to further safeguard plants from pests.

Vertical Gardening: 5. Increased accessibility: Vertical gardens can be designed at a height that minimizes bending and kneeling, making them more accessible for individuals with physical limitations or disabilities. This accessibility factor allows more people to engage in gardening and enjoy its benefits.

1. Utilization of unused spaces: Vertical gardening uses vertical surfaces that are often underutilized, such as walls, fences, or balconies. It allows you to convert these spaces into productive gardens, maximizing available areas and bringing greenery to unexpected places.
2. Diverse plant options: Vertical gardening opens up opportunities to grow a wider range of plants, including vining crops, flowers, and herbs that naturally thrive in a vertical orientation. This expands the variety of plants you can cultivate, enhancing the diversity and aesthetics of your garden.
3. Water conservation: Vertical gardens can be designed to be water-efficient. By incorporating techniques such as drip irrigation or hydroponics, water can be targeted directly to the plant roots, reducing water waste through evaporation or runoff.
4. Noise and air pollution reduction: Vertical gardens can act as natural filters, absorbing and reducing noise and air pollution. They create a barrier between buildings or roads and can help improve the air quality in urban environments.

Both raised beds and vertical gardening offer unique advantages for optimizing growing areas. Combined, they provide even greater benefits, allowing for efficient use of space, improved plant health, and increased yields. These techniques have become increasingly popular as people seek innovative solutions for gardening in limited spaces and urban environments.

Hydroponics and aquaponics: soilless gardening techniques

 Hydroponics and aquaponics are soilless gardening techniques that allow plants to grow in a controlled environment without using traditional soil. Instead, they rely on water and nutrient-rich solutions to provide the necessary elements for plant growth.
Hydroponics is a method of growing plants in water-based solutions supplemented with nutrients. The plants are usually placed in containers or beds filled with inert growing mediums like perlite, rock wool, or coconut coir to support their roots. Nutrients are dissolved in the water, and the plants receive them directly through their root systems. This method provides plants with an optimal balance of water, oxygen, and nutrients, leading to faster growth rates and higher yields. Hydroponics systems can be designed in various configurations, such as nutrient film technique (NFT), deep water culture (DWC), or aeroponics.
On the other hand, aquaponics is a combination of hydroponics and aquaculture. It involves the cultivation of plants and the rearing of fish in a

symbiotic environment. In an aquaponics system, fish are kept in tanks or ponds, and their waste produces ammonia-rich water. This water is then pumped into the hydroponic component of the system, where beneficial bacteria convert the ammonia into nitrates. The plants uptake these nitrates as nutrients, effectively filtering the water for the fish. The filtered water is then recirculated back to the fish tank, creating a closed-loop system. Aquaponics provides a sustainable and efficient way of growing both plants and fish, with the plants benefiting from the nutrient-rich water and the fish benefiting from the filtered and oxygenated water.

Both hydroponics and aquaponics offer several advantages over traditional soil-based gardening. They allow for year-round cultivation regardless of weather conditions and can be practised in urban environments where land space is limited. Since these methods provide precise control over the growing conditions, such as nutrient levels, pH, and light, they enable optimized plant growth and minimize the use of pesticides and fertilizers. Additionally, by eliminating the need for soil, issues such as soil-borne diseases and pests can be reduced.

However, it's important to note that hydroponics and aquaponics require careful monitoring and management of the water, nutrient levels, and overall system balance to ensure the success of the plants and the well-being of the fish in aquaponics setups. Nonetheless, these innovative soilless gardening techniques have gained popularity due to their efficiency, sustainability, and potential for high-yield crop production.

1. Hydroponics Techniques:
    - Nutrient Film Technique (NFT): In this method, a thin film of nutrient-rich water continuously flows over the roots of the plants, providing a constant supply of nutrients and oxygen.
    - Deep Water Culture (DWC): Plants are suspended in a nutrient solution with their roots submerged in the water. Air stones or diffusers are used to provide oxygen to the roots.
    - Aeroponics: The plants' roots are suspended in the air, and a fine mist of nutrient solution is sprayed onto the roots at regular intervals. This method maximizes oxygen availability to the roots.
1. Aquaponics Components:
    - Fish Tank: This is where fish are kept, and their waste is produced. The size and type of fish can vary depending on the system and its intended purpose.
    - Grow Beds: These are containers filled with a growing medium where plants are placed. The plants' roots grow into

    the growing medium and absorb the nutrients from the water.
    - Solids Removal: Aquaponics systems often include components such as settling tanks or mechanical filters to remove solid waste generated by the fish, preventing clogging and maintaining water quality.
1. System Benefits:
    - Water Conservation: Hydroponics and aquaponics use significantly less water than traditional soil-based gardening because water is recirculated within the system.
    - Efficient Nutrient Utilization: Nutrient solutions in hydroponics are precisely formulated, providing plants with the nutrients they need for optimal growth. Aquaponics utilizes the waste produced by fish as a natural fertilizer for plants.
    - Faster Growth and Higher Yields: With controlled conditions, plants in hydroponics and aquaponics grow faster and can achieve higher yields compared to traditional gardening methods.
    - Year-Round Cultivation: These techniques allow for year-round production regardless of seasonal

changes, providing a consistent supply of fresh produce.

1. Considerations:
   - Monitoring and Maintenance: Regular monitoring of pH levels, nutrient concentrations, and system components is crucial for successful operation.
   - System Balance: Maintaining a balanced ecosystem in aquaponics is important, as fish, plants, and bacteria rely on each other for a healthy system.
   - Energy Input: Hydroponics and aquaponics systems may require supplemental lighting, heating, or cooling, depending on the location and environmental conditions.

Both hydroponics and aquaponics offer innovative solutions for sustainable agriculture, enabling efficient and productive cultivation of a wide range of crops. These techniques continue to evolve with advancements in technology and our understanding of plant and fish interactions, further improving their efficiency and potential for widespread adoption.

Chapter 8: Extending the Growing Season

"Extending the growing season" refers to prolonging the period during which crops can be cultivated and harvested. In traditional farming, the growing season is determined by the natural climate conditions, including temperature, sunlight, and precipitation. However, with advancements in technology and agricultural techniques, it has become possible to extend the growing season beyond its natural limits.

There are several methods and strategies employed to extend the growing season:

1. Greenhouses: Greenhouses are structures made of transparent materials like glass or plastic that allow sunlight to enter while trapping heat inside. By controlling temperature, humidity, and other environmental factors, greenhouses create an artificial microclimate, enabling year-round cultivation. This technology allows farmers to grow crops that would otherwise be impossible in their local climate.

2. High Tunnels: High tunnels, also known as hoop houses, are unheated structures with plastic-covered frames that protect crops from adverse weather conditions. They act as mini-greenhouses, capturing solar energy

and creating a warmer environment. High tunnels are less expensive and easier to construct than traditional greenhouses, making them accessible to small-scale farmers.

3. Cold Frames: Cold frames are small, low-profile structures with transparent tops that capture sunlight and provide protection from cold temperatures and frost. They are often used for starting seedlings earlier in the spring or growing cold-tolerant crops during the winter months.
4. Row Covers: Row covers are lightweight, breathable fabrics placed directly over crops to protect them from frost, wind, and pests. They provide a few degrees of temperature protection and can extend the growing season by a few weeks, depending on the crop.
5. Crop Selection: Another way to extend the growing season is by selecting crop varieties that have shorter maturation periods or are more tolerant to colder temperatures. By choosing early-maturing or cold-tolerant varieties, farmers can start planting earlier in the spring or continue growing crops into the fall.

Extending the growing season can have various benefits. It allows farmers to increase their productivity and profitability by harvesting more crops throughout the year. It also provides a more consistent supply of fresh produce, reducing reliance on imports and improving food security. Additionally, it can contribute to sustainable agriculture practices by reducing the need for artificial inputs like pesticides and fertilizers.

However, it's important to note that extending the growing season requires careful management of resources, such as water and energy, to maintain the desired microclimate. It also requires additional investment in infrastructure and equipment. Nonetheless, extending the growing season is a valuable technique for modern agriculture with the potential for increased yields and the ability to cultivate a wider range of crops.

1. Season Extension Techniques: Various techniques can be employed to manipulate the growing environment and extend the season. These include using mulch to insulate the soil, utilizing raised beds to warm up the soil faster in the spring, employing thermal mass such as stones or water barrels to absorb and release heat, and employing windbreaks or shelter belts to protect crops from cold winds.
2. Hydroponics and Aquaponics: Hydroponics is a method of growing plants without soil, where the roots are submerged in a nutrient-rich water solution. Aquaponics combines hydroponics with aquaculture, where fish waste provides the nutrients for plant growth. These soil-less cultivation methods

can be practised indoors or in greenhouses, allowing year-round production.
3. Vertical Farming: Vertical farming involves growing crops in vertically stacked layers or racks using artificial lighting, temperature control, and hydroponic or aeroponic systems. By utilizing vertical space, this method maximizes land efficiency and can operate regardless of external climate conditions, extending the growing season indefinitely.
4. Heat Retention Techniques: To extend the growing season in colder climates, additional heat can be provided to crops. This can be achieved through techniques such as installing heating systems in greenhouses or using passive methods like composting, where decomposing organic matter generates heat that can warm the surrounding area.
5. Planting and Harvesting Techniques: By carefully timing the planting and harvesting of crops, farmers can optimize the growing season. This includes practices like succession planting, where new crops are planted as soon as previous ones are harvested, and staggered planting, where multiple plantings are done over time to ensure a continuous supply of fresh produce.

6. Season Extension Infrastructure: Alongside greenhouses and high tunnels, other infrastructure can be used to extend the growing season. Examples include cold storage facilities, root cellars, or controlled environment storage, which allow harvested crops to be stored for longer periods, ensuring availability even after the growing season ends.

These techniques can be used individually or in combination, depending on the specific needs and constraints of the farming operation. By extending the growing season, farmers can optimize production, increase income opportunities, and improve overall sustainability in agricultural practices.

Using season extenders like cold frames, row covers, and hoop houses

Using season extenders like cold frames, row covers, and hoop houses is a technique employed by gardeners and farmers to prolong the growing season for plants and protect them from adverse weather conditions.
1. Cold Frames: A cold frame is a simple structure with a transparent cover, typically made of glass or plastic, that allows sunlight to enter and trap heat inside. It acts as a mini-greenhouse and creates a microclimate

within the frame. Cold frames are typically placed directly on the ground or slightly elevated and can be used to start seeds earlier in the spring, protect delicate plants from frost, and continue growing plants later into the fall or winter. The trapped heat inside the cold frame helps to maintain higher temperatures than the outside environment, protecting the plants from cold temperatures and providing a sheltered environment for growth.

2. Row Covers: Row covers are lightweight, semi-transparent fabrics made of materials like floating row cover fabric, agricultural fleece, or polyethene. They are draped over plants and secured to the ground with stakes or weights. Row covers allow sunlight, air, and moisture to pass through while providing a protective barrier against pests, frost, wind, and excessive heat. They can be used to warm the soil and air, retain moisture, and create a shield against insect damage. Row covers are particularly useful for extending the growing season of sensitive crops, such as lettuce, spinach, and other cool-season vegetables.

3. Hoop Houses: Hoop houses, also known as high tunnels, are larger structures that resemble greenhouses but with a simpler design and lower cost. They consist of a series of hoops made of metal or PVC pipes

covered with a layer of greenhouse plastic. Hoop houses are typically taller than cold frames and provide a larger growing area. They offer protection from frost, wind, and excessive rain while allowing sunlight to penetrate and warm the interior. Hoop houses create a controlled environment that extends the growing season for various crops, including vegetables, fruits, and flowers. Farmers often use them to start plants earlier in the spring, grow crops during the winter, and protect sensitive plants from harsh weather conditions.

4. Cloches: Cloches are individual protective covers used to shield small plants or seedlings. They can be made of glass, plastic, or even inverted jars. Cloches are placed over individual plants, creating a mini-greenhouse effect by trapping heat and providing insulation. They protect plants from frost, wind, and pests, allowing sunlight to reach them. Cloches are useful for starting early crops or protecting tender plants in the early spring or late fall.

5. Low Tunnels: Low tunnels are similar to hoop houses but on a smaller scale. They consist of flexible hoops inserted into the ground along a row of plants, and a covering material such as greenhouse plastic or row cover fabric is draped over the hoops. Low tunnels provide protection and create a

warmer environment for plants, helping to extend the growing season. They are commonly used for cool-season vegetables and can be easily constructed and moved as needed.

6. Thermal Mass: Adding thermal mass, such as water containers or rocks, within season extender structures can help regulate temperature. Thermal mass absorbs heat during the day and releases it at night, providing a more stable and favourable growing environment. Water containers, in particular, have a high heat capacity and can act as a heat sink, moderating temperature fluctuations within the structure.
7. Ventilation: Proper ventilation is essential when using season extenders to prevent overheating and maintain optimal airflow. Most season extender structures have vents or openings that can be adjusted to regulate temperature and humidity. Ventilation helps prevent diseases, mould, and excessive moisture buildup, ensuring healthy plant growth.
8. Crop Selection: When using season extenders, choosing appropriate crops well-suited to the extended growing conditions is important. Cool-season crops, such as lettuce, spinach, radishes, and kale, are excellent choices for early spring and late fall planting. Understanding the specific

temperature and light requirements of different crops will help determine which ones are best suited for season extension.

By employing these techniques and strategies, gardeners and farmers can maximize their growing season, protect their plants from adverse weather, and enjoy a wider variety of fresh produce throughout the year. It requires careful planning, monitoring, and adjustments based on weather conditions. Still, the benefits of season extenders can be significant in terms of increased yield, plant health, and overall garden productivity.

Protecting plants from frost and extreme temperatures

Protecting plants from frost and extreme temperatures is an important aspect of gardening and agriculture, as these environmental conditions can be detrimental to plant health and survival. Frost and extreme temperatures can cause significant damage to plants by disrupting their cellular structure, damaging tissues, and inhibiting their metabolic processes. Therefore, implementing measures to protect plants from these conditions is crucial to ensure their well-being and productivity.

Here are some common methods used to protect plants from frost and extreme temperatures:

1. Covering: One of the simplest and most effective ways to protect plants from frost is by covering them. This can be done using various materials such as blankets, burlap, plastic sheets, or specialized frost protection fabrics. Covering the plants helps trap heat radiating from the ground and creates a slightly warmer microclimate than the surrounding environment. It is essential to securely anchor the covers to prevent them from blowing away and to remove them during the day to allow sunlight and air circulation.
2. Mulching: Applying a layer of mulch around the base of plants can help insulate the soil and protect plant roots from extreme temperature fluctuations. Organic materials like straw, leaves, wood chips, or compost can be used as mulch. Mulch acts as an insulating barrier, preventing the soil from rapidly losing heat and protecting the root zone.
3. Watering: Watering plants before a frost event can provide some protection. Water releases heat as it freezes, creating a minor warming effect for the plant. Additionally, moist soil retains heat better than dry soil, reducing the risk of freezing. However, this method should be used cautiously, as overwatering can adversely affect plant health.

4. Windbreaks: Strong winds can exacerbate the damaging effects of frost and cold temperatures on plants. Planting windbreaks, such as trees, shrubs, or fences, can help reduce the impact of wind by creating a barrier that deflects and slows down wind speed. This minimizes the cooling effect and provides some insulation for the plants.
5. Choosing appropriate plant varieties: Selecting plant varieties that are well-suited to the local climate and can withstand frost and extreme temperatures is an important preventive measure. Some plants are naturally more resistant to cold, while others are more susceptible. By choosing hardy varieties, gardeners can increase the chances of their plants surviving adverse weather conditions.
6. Cold frames and row cover: Cold frames and row covers provide additional protection to plants during colder months. Cold frames are enclosed boxes with transparent tops that allow sunlight to enter and create a warmer environment. Row covers are lightweight fabrics placed directly over the plants, creating a barrier against frost and cold temperatures while allowing sunlight and moisture to reach the plants.
7. Use of heat sources: In severely cold or prolonged freezing temperatures,

supplemental heat sources can be employed to raise the ambient temperature around plants. This can include using electric heaters, heat lamps, or even simple incandescent light bulbs placed strategically near the plants. However, caution must be exercised to prevent fire hazards or plant damage from direct contact with heat sources.

8. Plant placement and microclimates: Strategic placement of plants within the landscape can help create microclimates that offer protection from frost and extreme temperatures. For example, planting sensitive plants near structures, walls, or fences can provide added warmth by reflecting heat radiated from these surfaces. Similarly, planting on slopes or raised beds can improve air drainage and prevent cold air from settling around the plants.

9. Irrigation management: Proper irrigation practices can contribute to frost protection. Irrigating the soil thoroughly before a freeze can help prevent the plants from drying out, as moist soil retains heat better. However, it's important to avoid overwatering, as excess water can increase the risk of freezing. Additionally, timing irrigation so that plants are not wet when temperatures drop can prevent ice formation on plant surfaces, which can cause further damage.

10. Pruning and trimming: Pruning and trimming plants can help reduce their vulnerability to frost and extreme temperatures. Removing dead or damaged branches can improve the overall health and vigour of the plant, making it more resilient to cold stress. Pruning can also help open up the canopy, allowing better air circulation and reducing the risk of frost pockets forming.
11. Use of frost alarms and thermometers: Installing frost alarms or digital thermometers with frost sensors can provide real-time information about temperature drops. These devices can alert gardeners or farmers to impending frost events, allowing them to take immediate protective measures for their plants.
12. Cold-hardening techniques: Gradually exposing plants to cooler temperatures in the fall can help them develop cold-hardiness. This process, known as cold hardening, involves reducing watering, withholding fertilizer, and exposing the plants to slightly lower temperatures over time. Cold-hardened plants are better equipped to withstand frost and extreme temperatures.
13. Protective barriers: Physical barriers, such as wooden or plastic windbreaks, can be erected around vulnerable plants to

shield them from harsh winds and cold air. These barriers can help create a more favourable microclimate and provide an added layer of protection.

Remember, it's important to consider the specific needs and tolerances of different plant species when implementing these protective measures. By combining multiple strategies and adjusting them based on weather conditions, gardeners and farmers can significantly improve the chances of their plants surviving frost and extreme temperatures.

Harvesting techniques for mature and immature crops

Harvesting techniques vary depending on the maturity of the crops being harvested. Mature crops are those that have reached their full growth and are ready for harvesting, while immature crops are still in the early stages of growth and may not have fully developed their desired characteristics. Here are some common harvesting techniques for both mature and immature crops:

Harvesting Techniques for Mature Crops:
1. Hand Harvesting: This method involves manually picking mature crops by hand. It is commonly used for crops like fruits, vegetables, and some grains. Hand harvesting allows for selective picking,

ensuring only ripe crops are harvested, but it can be labour-intensive and time-consuming.
2. Mechanical Harvesting: In large-scale agriculture, mechanical harvesting is often employed for efficient and faster crop collection. Pieces of machinery, like combine harvesters, reapers, or pickers, are used to mechanically harvest crops such as grains, corn, and soybeans. Mechanical harvesting is generally suitable for crops with uniform maturity levels.
3. Tree Shaking: This technique is specifically used for fruit-bearing trees like apples, oranges, or peaches. Vibrating machines or devices are used to shake the tree's branches, causing ripe fruits to fall onto catch nets or onto the ground, where they can be collected.
4. Vineyard Harvesting: Vineyard crops like grapes are harvested by hand or mechanical means. Hand harvesting is often preferred for higher quality wines as it allows selective picking of the ripest grapes. Mechanical harvesting involves using specialized grape harvesters that gently shake the vines, causing the grapes to fall into collection bins.

Harvesting Techniques for Immature Crops:
1. Thinning: In the case of crops like carrots, radishes, or beets, thinning is a common

technique to promote proper growth and spacing. Immature plants are selectively removed, allowing the remaining plants to have adequate room to develop fully.

2. Baby Leaf Harvesting: For crops like lettuce, spinach, or herbs, the leaves can be harvested when they are still young and tender. Baby leaf harvesting involves selectively cutting off the outer leaves while leaving the inner leaves and the plant itself to continue growing for subsequent harvests.

3. Cut-and-Come-Again: This technique is commonly used for crops like kale or Swiss chard. Instead of uprooting the entire plant, only the outer leaves are harvested, allowing the inner leaves to continue growing. This way, multiple harvests can be obtained from the same plant.

4. Microgreens Harvesting: Microgreens are the young, tender shoots of various vegetables and herbs. They are harvested when they have developed their first true leaves, usually within 7-14 days of germination. The entire plant is typically cut just above the soil line for harvesting.

These are some examples of harvesting techniques for both mature and immature crops. The specific method used will depend on the type of crop, its maturity stage, and the desired quality and yield requirements.

Harvesting Techniques for Mature Crops: 5. Strip Harvesting: This method involves cutting or stripping the entire crop from the plant in one pass. It is commonly used for crops like wheat, barley, or oats. Harvesters with cutting mechanisms or blades remove the crop at ground level, separating the grains from the plant material.

1. Swathing: Swathing is a technique used for crops with long stems or plants that need to dry before further processing. The crop is cut and laid in rows on the field to dry. This is often done with crops like hay, oilseeds (such as canola), or forage crops like alfalfa. Once the crop has dried sufficiently, it can be baled or collected for further processing.
2. Pulling or Uprooting: Some crops, such as root vegetables like carrots, onions, or potatoes, require uprooting from the ground. This can be done manually or using machinery like a potato harvester. The plants are pulled or dug out, and the crop is separated from the foliage and soil.

Harvesting Techniques for Immature Crops: 5. Green Harvesting: In certain situations, it may be necessary to harvest crops before they reach full maturity due to various factors like disease, weather conditions, or market demand. Green harvesting involves selectively picking the crops while they are still immature but usable. This

technique is often employed for crops like green beans or peas.
1. Top Harvesting: Some crops, such as sugar beets or turnips, are harvested by removing the top portion of the plant, leaving the root or bulb in the ground. The tops are typically cut off, and the remaining root or bulb is left to be harvested at a later stage.
2. Tipping or Topping: Tipping or topping is commonly used for crops like tobacco, sunflowers, or some types of flowers. It involves removing the upper part of the plant to promote the development of lateral shoots or flowers. This technique encourages the production of side shoots or blooms, resulting in increased yield or desired characteristics.

It's important to note that specific harvesting techniques can vary based on regional practices, crop types, and local conditions. Farmers and agricultural professionals often adapt their harvesting methods based on their experience, resources, and the specific requirements of the crops they cultivate.

Chapter 9: Harvesting and Storing Your Produce

Harvesting and storing your produce is an essential part of gardening and farming. It involves collecting the fruits, vegetables, or other crops you have grown and then suitably preserving them to maintain their freshness, flavour, and nutritional value for as long as possible. Here are the key steps involved in harvesting and storing produce:

1. Timing: Harvesting should be done at the right time when the crops are mature and ready for consumption. This timing varies depending on the type of produce. For example, fruits are usually harvested when they reach full ripeness, while vegetables are often harvested when they are young and tender.

2. Harvesting techniques: Different crops require specific harvesting techniques. Some products can be simply handpicked, such as tomatoes or berries, while others may need to be cut or dug up from the ground, like root vegetables or tubers. It's important to use the appropriate tools and methods to avoid crop damage during harvesting.

3. Handling: Proper handling during and after harvesting is crucial to maintain the quality

of the produce. Care should be taken to avoid bruising, crushing, or damaging the fruits and vegetables. Delicate produce should be handled gently and not exposed to excessive heat or sunlight, as this can accelerate spoilage.

4. Cleaning: After harvesting, it's important to clean the product to remove dirt, debris, and any potential contaminants. This can be done by gently rinsing the crops with clean water. However, some fruits and vegetables should not be washed until just before use, as excess moisture can lead to faster deterioration.

5. Sorting and grading: Sorting involves separating the harvested produce based on size, shape, colour, or any other quality criteria. This helps identify damaged or spoiled items that should be consumed or processed first. Grading is often done for commercial purposes, where produce is categorized into different quality grades for market distribution.

6. Storage conditions: Proper storage conditions play a crucial role in preserving the freshness and quality of harvested produce. Factors such as temperature, humidity, and light exposure can significantly affect the shelf life of different crops. Some fruits and vegetables require refrigeration, while others can be stored at

room temperature. It's important to research the ideal storage conditions for each type of produce.
7. Packaging: Packaging your harvested produce appropriately helps protect it from physical damage, moisture loss, and exposure to air. Use breathable containers, such as mesh bags or perforated plastic bags, to allow air circulation and prevent excess moisture buildup. Avoid overcrowding the containers, as this can lead to bruising and spoilage.
8. Preservation methods: If you have an abundant harvest and want to extend the shelf life of your produce, you can consider various preservation methods. These include canning, freezing, drying, pickling, or fermenting, depending on the type of produce. Each preservation method has specific requirements and steps to follow.
9. Regular monitoring: It's important to inspect your stored produce for any signs of spoilage, rot, or pests. Remove any damaged or spoiled items promptly to prevent the spread of decay to the rest of the produce.
10. Ripening: Some fruits and vegetables continue to ripen after they are harvested. For example, tomatoes, bananas, and avocados can be harvested when they are slightly underripe and left to ripen at room temperature. Be sure to check the specific

ripening requirements of each crop and monitor them closely to avoid overripening or spoilage.

11. Removing excess foliage: When harvesting certain crops like root vegetables or leafy greens, it's a good practice to remove excess foliage or stems. This reduces moisture loss from the harvested portion and helps prolong its shelf life.

12. Curing: Curing is a process often used for root vegetables, such as onions, garlic, and potatoes. It involves drying the freshly harvested crops in a warm, well-ventilated area for some time. Curing helps toughen the outer layers, enhances flavour, and extends storage life.

13. Storage location: Choose a suitable storage location for your produce. It should have the right temperature, humidity, and ventilation. Ideally, the storage area should be cool, dark, and well-ventilated to minimize spoilage. Avoid storing produce near sources of ethylene gas, such as ripening fruits, as ethylene can accelerate the ripening and decay of other produce.

14. Rotation: Implement a rotation system when storing your produce. Consume or use the oldest harvested items first to prevent spoilage and waste. This ensures that you enjoy your produce at its

peak freshness while minimizing losses due to spoilage.
15. Record-keeping: Maintain a record of the harvested and stored produce. This includes the harvest dates, storage methods, and any spoilage or quality change observations. This information can help you assess the effectiveness of your storage techniques and make improvements for future harvests.
16. Research crop-specific requirements: Different crops have specific requirements for harvesting and storage. Some fruits and vegetables are more sensitive to temperature, humidity, or ethylene exposure than others. Research the specific needs of each crop you grow to ensure optimal harvesting and storage practices.
17. Consider root cellar storage: If you have a root cellar or a cool, dark basement, you can utilize these spaces for storing certain types of produce. Root cellars provide a stable temperature and humidity environment that is beneficial for storing root vegetables, winter squash, and other crops that prefer cooler conditions.
18. Regularly check stored produce: Even with the best storage conditions, it's important to regularly check on your stored produce. Inspect them for any signs of decay, mould, or pests. Remove any spoiled

items immediately to prevent the spread of spoilage to other produce.
Remember, each crop has its unique requirements, so it's essential to do some research and understand the specific needs of the fruits and vegetables you are harvesting. By following proper harvesting and storage practices, you can enjoy the fruits of your labour for an extended period and minimize food waste.

Harvesting vegetables at their peak flavour and maturity

Harvesting vegetables at their peak flavour and maturity refers to picking vegetables from plants when they have reached their optimal ripeness and taste. This ensures that the vegetables are at their best in terms of flavour, texture, and nutritional content.
The timing of harvest is crucial because vegetables undergo changes in taste, texture, and nutritional composition as they grow and mature. Harvesting too early may result in underdeveloped flavours and textures while harvesting too late can lead to overripe vegetables that are past their prime.
Farmers and gardeners consider various factors such as colour, size, texture, and aroma to determine the peak flavour and maturity of vegetables. Different vegetables have different indicators of readiness for harvest. For example, tomatoes are often picked when they are fully ripe

and have a deep colour and a slight give when gently squeezed. On the other hand, leafy greens like lettuce and spinach are typically harvested when they are young and tender before they become too mature and develop a bitter taste.

Harvesting at the right time enhances the taste and quality of vegetables and ensures that they are at their nutritional peak. As vegetables mature, their nutrient content changes. For instance, vitamin C levels may decrease as vegetables ripen, so harvesting them when fully mature ensures that they retain the highest nutrient content possible.

Harvesting at the peak flavour and maturity also helps to maximize the yield. By harvesting vegetables when they are at their best, farmers can provide consumers with high-quality produce that is flavorful and enjoyable to eat. This practice is especially important for farmers selling directly to consumers at farmers' markets or through community-supported agriculture (CSA) programs, where the quality and taste of the vegetables can significantly impact customer satisfaction and repeat business.

1. Observation and experience: Harvesting vegetables at their peak requires experience and close observation of the plants. Farmers and gardeners develop an understanding of each vegetable variety, noting the changes in appearance, texture, and aroma as the vegetables progress towards maturity.

2. Taste testing: Taste testing is an essential tool for determining the optimal time for harvest. Farmers or gardeners sample the vegetables regularly to assess their flavour development. This hands-on approach allows them to gauge the sweetness, tenderness, and overall taste of the vegetables.
3. Texture and firmness: The texture and firmness of a vegetable can indicate its maturity. For example, cucumbers are typically harvested when they are firm and crisp, while zucchinis are best picked when they are still tender and have smooth skin.
4. Colour and appearance: The colour and appearance of vegetables can indicate their readiness for harvest. Some vegetables, like bell peppers, change colour as they mature, transitioning from green to red, yellow, or orange. Others, such as eggplants, develop a glossy sheen when fully ripe.
5. Harvesting in the morning: Many farmers prefer to harvest vegetables in the morning when the temperatures are cooler. This helps to preserve the freshness and quality of the product by reducing the risk of wilting or damage from the heat of the day.
6. Post-harvest handling: Proper post-harvest handling is crucial to maintain the flavour and quality of vegetables. After harvest, handling the vegetables carefully is

important avoiding any bruising or damage. Cooling the vegetables promptly and storing them at the appropriate temperature and humidity levels can help to preserve their flavour and nutritional content.
7. Variations in maturity: It's worth noting that not all vegetables reach their peak flavour and maturity at the same time. Different cultivars and varieties may have specific requirements and indicators for optimal harvest. Additionally, some vegetables, such as radishes or baby greens, are harvested early to capture their delicate flavours and textures.

By following these guidelines and paying close attention to the specific characteristics of each vegetable, farmers and gardeners can ensure that they harvest vegetables at their peak flavour and maturity. This approach results in produce that not only tastes delicious but also provides maximum nutritional benefits to those who consume them.

Proper washing, drying, and storage methods

Proper washing, drying, and storage methods are essential to maintain the cleanliness, quality, and longevity of various items such as clothing, dishes, and food. Here's an explanation of these methods:

1. Washing: When it comes to washing items, such as clothes or dishes, the following steps can be followed:
- Read the manufacturer's instructions: Check the care labels or user manuals for any specific washing instructions provided by the manufacturer. This will ensure you follow the recommended cleaning method.
- Sort items: Sort your laundry or dishes based on colour, fabric type, or level of dirtiness. Separating items helps prevent colour bleeding, damage, or contamination.
- Pre-treat stains: Before washing, treat any stains or spots on the items. Follow the recommended stain removal techniques for the specific type of stain.
- Select the appropriate detergent: Choose a detergent suitable for the item being washed. Some items require gentle detergents, while others may need specialized products such as dishwashing liquid or fabric softener.
- Follow the recommended temperature: Pay attention to the temperature recommendations for washing. Hot water is usually suitable for white clothes or heavily soiled items, while cold or lukewarm water may be preferable for delicate fabrics.
- Use proper washing techniques: Follow the recommended washing cycle, and avoid overcrowding the washing machine or sink.

Agitate or scrub gently to avoid damaging the items.
1. Drying: After washing, proper drying techniques ensure that items are fully dried without damage or excessive wrinkles. Here are some key points:
- Check the manufacturer's instructions: Review the care labels or user manuals for drying recommendations. Some items may require air-drying, while others can be machine-dried.
- Air-drying: If air-drying is recommended, lay the item flat or hang it up in a well-ventilated area. Avoid direct sunlight to prevent colour fading.
- Machine drying: If machine drying is allowed, select the appropriate drying cycle and temperature. Avoid using high heat for delicate items to prevent shrinking or damage. Remove items promptly to minimize wrinkles.
1. Storage: Proper storage methods help preserve the condition and extend the lifespan of various items. Consider the following tips:
- Clean and dry thoroughly: Ensure that items are clean and completely dry before storing them. Moisture can lead to mould, mildew, or musty odours.
- Fold or hang items appropriately: For clothing, fold items neatly to prevent

creasing or misshaping. Hang delicate or easily wrinkled clothes to maintain their shape.
- Use suitable containers: Store items in containers or organizers designed for their specific purpose. This can include garment bags for clothes, airtight containers for food, or stackable containers for dishes.
- Keep away from damaging factors: Store items away from direct sunlight, extreme temperatures, humidity, pests, or chemicals that could cause damage or deterioration.

By following these proper washing, drying, and storage methods, you can help ensure your items' cleanliness, quality, and longevity. Always refer to the specific guidelines provided by the manufacturer for the best care practices.

1. Washing:
- Water temperature: In addition to following temperature recommendations, consider using cold water for dark-coloured clothes to prevent fading or bleeding of dyes. Warm or hot water is often used for heavily soiled items or whites.
- Hand-washing: Some delicate items may require hand-washing instead of machine washing. Fill a basin or sink with lukewarm water and a gentle detergent, agitate the item gently and rinse thoroughly.
- Delicate fabrics: Take extra care when washing delicate fabrics such as silk, lace, or

cashmere. Consider using a mesh laundry bag or pillowcase to protect them during machine washing.
- Fasteners and zippers: Before washing, close zippers, fasten buttons, and secure any hooks or clasps to prevent them from snagging or damaging other items.

1. Drying:
- Air-drying tips: When air-drying clothes, consider using a drying rack or laying them flat on a clean, dry surface. Reshape garments if necessary to maintain their original form.
- Tumble drying: If using a dryer, check the item's care label for any restrictions on tumble drying. Some fabrics may require a low heat setting or air-only cycle to avoid damage.
- Shrinkage prevention: To minimize the risk of shrinking, avoid over-drying clothes in the dryer. Remove them while slightly damp, as they will continue to dry naturally.
- Ironing: If ironing is necessary, follow the recommended ironing instructions for each fabric type. Use the appropriate heat setting and place a cloth or ironing sheet between the item and the iron to prevent direct heat damage.

1. Storage:
- Clothing storage: Fold clothes neatly or use hangers to prevent wrinkles and maintain

their shape. Consider using dividers or organizers within drawers or closets to maximize space and keep items organized.
- Shoe storage: Store shoes in a cool, dry place away from direct sunlight. Use shoe racks or boxes to prevent scuffing and maintain their condition. Stuffing shoes with tissue paper or using shoe trees helps retain their shape.
- Food storage: Store food in airtight containers or resealable bags to maintain freshness and prevent contamination. Label containers with the contents and date to easily track expiration dates.
- Seasonal storage: When storing items not in use, clean and prepare them properly. For example, clean and oil gardening tools or winterize outdoor equipment to protect them from the elements.
- Document storage: Keep important documents in a safe, dry place, preferably in a fireproof and waterproof container. Consider using acid-free sleeves or folders to prevent yellowing or deterioration.

Remember, specific items may have unique washing, drying, and storage requirements, so always refer to the manufacturer's instructions or consult a professional if you're unsure.

Canning, freezing, and drying techniques for preserving your harvest

Canning, freezing, and drying are three common techniques for preserving food harvests. These methods help extend the shelf life of fruits, vegetables, and other perishable food items, allowing you to enjoy them for an extended period. Here's an explanation of each technique:

1. Canning: Canning involves sealing food in airtight containers (usually glass jars) to prevent the growth of bacteria, yeast, or mould that can cause spoilage. The process typically involves heating the food to a high temperature to kill microorganisms, followed by sealing the jars. There are two main canning methods: water bath and pressure canning.
    - Water bath canning: This method is suitable for high-acid foods like fruits, tomatoes, pickles, and jams. The food is packed into sterilized jars, covered with a liquid (such as syrup or juice), and then immersed in a pot of boiling water for a specified time. The heat kills bacteria and creates a vacuum seal as the jars cool down.
    - Pressure canning: This method is necessary for low-acid foods like vegetables, meats, and soups that require higher temperatures to eliminate harmful bacteria, such as

botulinum. The food is packed into jars, sealed, and then processed in a pressure canner at specific temperatures and pressures to ensure food safety.

1. Freezing: Freezing is a popular method for preserving a wide range of foods, including fruits, vegetables, meats, seafood, and prepared meals. Freezing works by lowering the temperature of the food to inhibit the growth of microorganisms. It slows down enzyme activity, which helps retain the food's quality, flavour, and nutritional value.

To freeze food effectively, it's important to follow a few steps. First, prepare the food by cleaning, peeling, and cutting it into appropriate sizes. Blanching (briefly boiling or steaming) vegetables before freezing helps retain their texture and colour. Next, package the food in freezer-safe containers or bags, removing excess air to prevent freezer burn. Label the packages with the date and contents for easy identification. Finally, place the packaged food in a freezer set to 0°F (-18°C) or below for long-term storage.

1. Drying: Drying, also known as dehydration, involves removing moisture from food to inhibit the growth of bacteria, yeast, and mould. It is a suitable method for preserving fruits, vegetables, herbs, meats, and some dairy products. When properly dried, the

food becomes lightweight and compact and has a longer shelf life.

There are various techniques for drying food. Air drying or sun drying involves placing food in a well-ventilated area, protected from insects and dust, and allowing natural air circulation to evaporate moisture over time. Oven drying utilizes low heat (usually between 140°F to 160°F or 60°C to 70°C) to gradually dry the food. Dehydrators are electrical appliances designed specifically for drying food and offering more precise temperature and airflow control.

It's essential to ensure the food is adequately dried to prevent spoilage. The drying time varies depending on the food type, size, and moisture content. Once dried, store the food in airtight containers, preferably in a cool, dark, and dry place, to maintain quality.

Canning:
- Before scanning, it's crucial to start with fresh, high-quality produce. Discard any damaged or spoiled items.
- The canning process involves sterilizing jars and lids to ensure they are bacteria-free. This can be done by boiling them in water or using a dishwasher with a sanitizing cycle.
- In water bath canning, jars are completely submerged in boiling water and processed for a specific amount of time, which varies depending on the recipe and altitude. This

method is suitable for acidic foods with a pH of 4.6 or below.
- Pressure canning is necessary for low-acid foods with a pH above 4.6. The higher temperature achieved in a pressure canner (usually around 240°F or 116°C) ensures the destruction of harmful microorganisms like Clostridium botulinum.
- It's important to follow tested and approved canning recipes to ensure food safety. These recipes provide precise instructions on processing times, ingredients, and proper canning procedures.
- Properly canned foods can be stored in a cool, dark place for up to a year or longer, depending on the food.

Freezing:
- Freezing helps to preserve the quality, texture, and nutritional value of many foods.
- For optimal results, blanch vegetables before freezing. Blanching involves briefly immersing vegetables in boiling water or steam and immediately cooling them in ice water. Blanching helps to inactivate enzymes that can cause loss of flavour, colour, and texture.
- Packaging foods properly is important to prevent freezer burn and maintain quality. Use freezer-safe bags or containers and remove as much air as possible from the

packaging to minimize oxidation and moisture loss.
- Label each package with the contents and date of freezing to keep track of the storage time.
- Most fruits and vegetables can be frozen for several months, but the storage time varies depending on the food. Generally, meats and poultry can be stored for 6 to 12 months, while prepared dishes or leftovers can be stored for 2 to 3 months.

Drying:
- Drying removes moisture from food, inhibiting the growth of microorganisms and preventing spoilage.
- Thinly sliced or small pieces of food dry more quickly and evenly than larger pieces.
- Air drying requires a well-ventilated area with low humidity. You can use racks, screens, or mesh trays to allow air circulation around the food.
- Oven drying is an alternative method if you don't have access to outdoor space or a food dehydrator. Keep the oven temperature low (around 140°F to 160°F or 60°C to 70°C) and prop the oven door open slightly to allow moisture to escape.
- Food dehydrators offer precise temperature and airflow control, making them an efficient option for drying food. Follow the

manufacturer's instructions for optimal results.
- Properly dried food should be leathery, brittle, or crisp, depending on the item. Moisture content should be low enough to prevent spoilage but not so low that the food becomes overly dry.
- Store dried food in airtight containers in a cool, dark, and dry place. The shelf life varies depending on the food, but properly dried items can often be stored for several months or even years.

Remember, each preservation method has its requirements and considerations. It's important to research specific guidelines and recipes for the particular foods you want to preserve to ensure safe and successful preservation.

Chapter 10: Enjoying Your Year-Round Harvest

"Enjoying Your Year-Round Harvest" refers to growing and harvesting various crops throughout the year, regardless of the seasonal limitations. It involves utilizing various techniques, tools, and strategies to extend the growing season and maximize the yield of fresh produce.

There are several methods and approaches to achieve a year-round harvest, including:

1. Greenhouses: Greenhouses provide a controlled environment that protects plants from extreme weather conditions and allows for year-round cultivation. By regulating temperature, humidity, and light, growers can create optimal conditions for plants to thrive. This enables the cultivation of crops that are typically restricted to specific seasons.

2. High Tunnels: High tunnels, also known as hoop houses or polytunnels, are simpler structures compared to greenhouses. They consist of a metal or plastic frame covered with a transparent material like polyethene. High tunnels provide some degree of climate control and protection from the elements, allowing for an extended growing season.

3. Cold Frames: Cold frames are small, enclosed structures with transparent tops that

capture and retain heat from the sun. They are typically placed close to a building or against a south-facing wall to maximize warmth. Cold frames are particularly useful for starting seedlings early in the season and growing cold-hardy crops during the winter months.

4. Indoor Growing Systems: Indoor gardening setups, such as hydroponics, aeroponics, and vertical farming, enable year-round cultivation without relying on natural sunlight or soil. These systems use artificial lighting, nutrient solutions, and controlled environments to grow plants efficiently. Indoor growing allows for precise control over environmental factors, resulting in consistent yields throughout the year.

5. Crop Selection and Succession Planting: Choosing the right crops and employing succession planting techniques can help maintain a continuous harvest. By selecting varieties with varying maturity times, growers can stagger planting dates to ensure a constant supply of fresh produce. As one crop nears harvest, another can be planted, maximizing available space and resources.

6. Season Extension Techniques: Various season extension techniques, such as row covers, mulching, and cloches, can protect plants from frost and extend the growing season. These methods trap heat, create

microclimates, and shield crops from harsh weather conditions, allowing for earlier planting in spring and later harvesting in fall.

Combining these methods and tailoring them to specific climates and growing conditions makes it possible to enjoy a diverse and abundant harvest throughout the year. Year-round gardening provides a steady supply of fresh, homegrown produce and reduces reliance on external food sources and promotes sustainability and self-sufficiency.

1. Crop Planning: Strategic crop planning is essential for a continuous harvest. Consider the time each crop matures, its growth requirements, and its compatibility with the available growing methods. Plan your planting schedule to ensure a smooth transition between crops and maintain a consistent supply.
2. Seasonal Crop Rotation: Implementing a crop rotation schedule helps manage soil fertility, control pests and diseases, and optimize yields. Rotate crops based on their nutritional needs and their impact on soil health. For example, legumes enrich the soil with nitrogen, while light feeders like leafy greens can follow heavy feeders like tomatoes.
3. Succession Planting: Succession planting involves regularly sowing or transplanting

new crops to replace harvested ones. This technique maximizes the use of available space and extends the growing season. As one crop reaches maturity, another is ready to take its place, ensuring a continuous supply of fresh produce.

4. Storing and Preserving Harvest: To enjoy your year-round harvest beyond its growing season, consider preserving and storing your produce. Techniques like canning, freezing, drying, fermenting, and pickling allow you to enjoy your homegrown fruits and vegetables during months when they aren't readily available.

5. Crop Varieties and Breeding: Explore different crop varieties that are specifically bred for extended growing seasons or cold tolerance. Look for varieties that have shorter maturity times, disease resistance, or the ability to withstand fluctuations in temperature. This way, you can maximize your chances of a successful year-round harvest.

6. Vertical Gardening: Utilize vertical space by growing plants vertically, such as on trellises, stakes, or wall-mounted systems. Vertical gardening maximizes the use of space and allows for a greater number of plants in a smaller area. It is particularly beneficial when working with limited space or in urban environments.

7. Microgreens and Sprouting: Microgreens are young, tender plants harvested shortly after germination, usually within two weeks. Sprouting involves germinating seeds and consuming the resulting young shoots. Both microgreens and sprouts can be grown indoors throughout the year, providing a quick and nutrient-rich addition to meals.
8. Overwintering Perennial Crops: Perennial crops, such as certain herbs, fruits, and vegetables, can survive winter and regrow in the following season. By understanding the overwintering requirements of these plants and providing proper protection, you can enjoy their harvest year after year.

Remember that the specific techniques and methods employed for year-round gardening may vary depending on your climate, available resources, and personal preferences. It's important to experiment, adapt, and learn from your experiences to optimize your year-round harvest.

Made in the USA
Middletown, DE
26 December 2024